TOP 10
SYDNEY

STEVE WOMERSLEY
RACHEL NEUSTEIN

EYEWITNESS TRAVEL

Left **Mosaic at St Mary's Cathedral** Centre **Sailing on Sydney Harbour** Right **Kings Cross**

LONDON, NEW YORK,
MELBOURNE, MUNICH AND DELHI
www.dk.com

Reproduced by Colourscan, Singapore

Printed and bound in China by
Leo Paper Products Ltd

First published in Great Britain in 2005
by Dorling Kindersley Limited 80 Strand, London
WC2R 0RL
A Penguin Company

Reprinted with revisions 2006, 2007, 2009
Copyright 2005, 2009 © Dorling Kindersley
Limited, London

All rights reserved. No part of this publication
may be reproduced, stored
in a retrieval system, or transmitted in
any form or by any means, electronic,
mechanical, photocopying, recording or
otherwise, without the prior written permission
of the copyright owner.

A CIP catalogue record is available from the
British Library.

ISBN 978 1 40532 379 6

Within each Top 10 list in this book, no hierarchy
of quality or popularity is implied. All 10 are, in
the editor's opinion, of roughly equal merit.

Floors are referred to throughout in accordance
with Australian usage; ie the "first floor" is the
floor above ground level.

We're trying to be cleaner and greener:
• we recycle waste and switch things off
• we use paper from responsibly managed
forests whenever possible
• we ask our printers to actively reduce
water and energy consumption
• we check out our suppliers' working
conditions – they never use child labour
**Find out more about our values and
best practices at www.dk.com**

Contents

Sydney's Top 10

The information in this DK Eyewitness Top 10 Travel Guide is checked regularly.
Every effort has been made to ensure that this book is as up-to-date as possible at the time of
going to press. Some details, however, such as telephone numbers, opening hours, prices,
gallery hanging arrangements and travel information are liable to change. The publishers
cannot accept responsibility for any consequences arising from the use of this book, nor for
any material on third party websites, and cannot guarantee that any website address in this
book will be a suitable source of travel information. We value the views and suggestions of
our readers very highly. Please write to: Publisher, DK Eyewitness Travel Guides,
Dorling Kindersley, 80 Strand, London, Great Britain WC2R 0RL.

Cover: Front – **Getty Images:** Stuart Westmorland bl; **Hemisphere Images:** Bruno Perousse main. Back –
Alamy Images: World Pictures tc; **DK Images:** Max Alexander tr; Rob Reichenfeld tl. Spine: **DK Images:**
Alan Williams b.

All prices in this guide are in Australian dollars

Left **Beare Park** Centre **Sydney Opera House & Sydney Harbour Bridge** Right **Shelly Beach**

Left **Victorian terrace house** Right **Botanic Gardens**

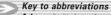
Key to abbreviations
Adm *admission charge* **Dis access** *disabled access*

3

SYDNEY'S
TOP 10

SYDNEY'S TOP 10

Sydney's Highlights

Sydney is blessed with stunning ocean beaches, magnificent national parks and a wonderful subtropical climate that makes the great outdoors irresistible to its four million inhabitants. The Eora people, the Aborigines who settled around Sydney Harbour, arrived approximately 50,000 years ago, while the white settlers arrived just over 200 years ago. Free settlers soon followed in the wake of the First Fleet of transported convicts, and after them several waves of migrants seeking a new life. Now, over two centuries later, the once far-flung penal colony has matured into a culturally diverse, tolerant and mesmerising city. Ideally located on the world's most beautiful harbour, Sydney is as exciting and bustling as it is laid back and relaxing.

1 Sydney Opera House

Sydney's architectural icon and world-renowned performing arts venue enjoys the most spectacular setting of any cultural institution in the world. It is the city's most popular tourist attraction *(see pp8–11)*.

2 Sydney Harbour Bridge

This enormous and beautiful structure was an economic and engineering triumph. It reshaped Sydney's landscape and lifted the city's spirits during the dark days of the Great Depression *(see pp12–13)*.

3 Sydney Harbour

From its pristine beaches to its working docklands, this deep-water port at the heart of this maritime city is the world's finest *(see pp14–17)*.

Previous pages: **Circular Quay**

4 The Rocks & Circular Quay

Governor Phillip and the First Fleet arrived here in 1788 to lay the foundations for Australia's white settlement. Now it's an engaging historic precinct and a lively transport hub *(see pp18–19)*.

5 Botanic Gardens & The Domain

This lovely green belt east of the city centre incorporates the Botanic Gardens and the Art Gallery of New South Wales, and has been one of Sydney's best-loved public spaces for almost 200 years *(see pp20–23)*.

6 Art Gallery of New South Wales

Boasting one of the country's most extensive collections of Australian and international art, this striking building in The Domain is not to be missed *(see pp24–7)*.

7 Darling Harbour & Chinatown

Chinatown's authentic bustle and flavour is the perfect counterpoint to the ritzy Darling Harbour precinct. An extension of the city centre, Darling Harbour offers numerous museums, bars, cafés and tourist attractions *(see pp28–9)*.

8 Powerhouse Museum

Kooky. Challenging. Hands-on. And plenty of fun. Powerhouse's eclectic and sometimes eccentric science and design collection appeals to children and adults alike *(see pp30–31)*.

Sydney Harbour

9 Taronga Zoo

The zoo's collection of Australian and exotic animals, not to mention its gorgeous setting overlooking the harbour, makes it a must-see destination for visitors *(see pp32–3)*.

10 Bondi Beach

Sydney's swimmers, surfers and sybarites all love Australia's most iconic beach. Don't leave the city without spending some time here, body surfing, walking along the clifftops or working on your tan *(see pp34–5)*.

🔟 Sydney Opera House

The Opera House's magnificent harbourside location, stunning architecture and excellent programme of events make it Sydney's number one destination. The modern masterpiece reflects the genius of its 1966 architect, Jørn Utzon. In 1999, Utzon agreed to prepare a guide of design principles for future changes to the building. This was welcome news for all who marvel at his masterpiece and for the four million visitors to the site each year.

Opera Theatre
Home to The Australian Ballet, the Sydney Dance Company and Opera Australia, this lovely theatre *(above)* seats more than 1,500. It hosted the site's first performance in 1973, Prokofiev's *War and Peace*.

Opera House roof tiles

🍷 After the show, kick back to live jazz and a late supper at the Opera Bar.

🎭 A range of performance packages is available.

- *Map N1*
- *Bennelong Point*
- *Open daily; Box Office open 9am–8:30pm Mon–Sat, 2 hrs prior to performances on Sun*
- *9250 7777; for hearing impaired 9250 7347*
- *www. sydneyopera house.com*
- *Essential tour: 9250 7250 (1 hour every 30 mins from 9am–5pm daily, $35); Backstage Tour (2 hours, from 7am, includes breakfast in Greenroom, $140)*
- *Dis access, loop, infra-red hearing systems and audio description service: 9250 7185*
- *Opera Bar: 9247 1666*

Top 10 Features

1. Roof
2. Concert Hall
3. Opera Theatre
4. Drama Theatre
5. Playhouse
6. The Studio
7. Walkways
8. Forecourt & Monumental Steps
9. Northern Foyers
10. Bars & Restaurants

Roof
Comprised of 10 "sails", the roof *(above)* is made of over one million tiles. Designed to counter the sunlight, the ceramic tiles take on a lustrous glow at dawn and dusk.

Concert Hall
The Opera House's most impressive venue, and home to the Sydney Symphony, seats 2,679 and hosts concerts, opera *(right)* and drama performances. Its acoustics are acclaimed worldwide, and the Grand Organ took ten years to design and tune.

Opera House and the Bridge

Drama Theatre
This intimate theatre was not part of Utzon's original plan. Today, however, it is a much-loved venue and its size ensures good sightlines from every seat.

➡ *One of the best vantage points for Opera House photographs is Mrs Macquarie's Chair (see pp20–21) at dawn.*

5 Playhouse
This intimate venue hosts contemporary theatre productions and the popular 'Kids at the House' programme.

8 Forecourt & Monumental Steps
Framed by the Botanic Gardens and Government House, the Forecourt and the 86-m (282-ft) wide Monumental Steps *(left)* are the perfect setting for outdoor events, such as ballroom dancing or Greek folk music. A weekly arts and crafts market is also held here.

10 Bars & Restaurants
Dining at Sydney Opera House caters for all tastes, from cocktails at the Opera Bar and snacks and light meals at the Sidewalk Café or Café West to a night of indulgence at the award-winning Guillaume at Bennelong *(see below & p58)*.

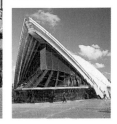

6 The Studio
The Opera House's grooviest and most flexible venue is The Studio. Staged here are contemporary short-run productions that include gay cabaret, hip-hop theatre, world music and country and western. Comedy and dance shows are also held here.

7 High Tea
High tea combines a 20-minute opera recital by some of the world's greatest opera singers with cuisine prepared by renowned chef Guillaume Brahimi, in the intimate Bennelong restaurant. High Tea at the Opera House takes place every Wednesday 2–4pm.

9 Northern Foyers
Topaz-tinted glass canopies and massive girders enclose the Northern Foyers of the Concert Hall and Opera Theatre, and offer spectacular 180-degree views of the harbour.

Bennelong
Governor Arthur Phillip built a home on the headland for his Aboriginal translator, Bennelong, and in 1792 Phillip took Bennelong back to London with him. When Bennelong returned to Australia in 1795 he found himself caught between cultures, and his drinking, womanising and violent outbursts became legendary, ending tragically in 1813. In 1817 a fort designed by Francis Greenway was built on the point named for Bennelong. It was replaced by a tram depot in 1902.

The arts and crafts market at the Forecourt is held every Sunday from 9am–4pm, subject to weather.

Left **Roof in mid-construction** Center **Completed roof** Right **The Red Book**

Raising the Roof

1954
Eugene Goosens, the Conservatorium of Music's director, lobbies the state Labour Premier, Joseph Cahill, to construct an opera house. Cahill appoints Goosens to a committee investigating the proposal.

1956
Upon his return from an overseas conducting tour, customs agents mysteriously find "pornography" in Sir Eugene's luggage. He resigns and returns to Europe leaving an overwrought and self-righteous media frenzy in his wake.

1957
A Danish architect, Jørn Utzon, is declared the project's architect. Utzon's prize money is £5,000. Projected cost of the project: $7 million. Projected completion date: 1963.

1958
Demolition of the old tram sheds on Bennelong Point commences. Following an unsuccessful fund-raising venture, the government establishes the Opera House Lottery to cover the estimated costs of construction.

1959
Premier Cahill responds to public and media concern about project delays and rising costs. He insists that work commence. Utzon and the project engineer

Ove Arup protest, asserting their plans are incomplete. Cahill dies in October 1959. Work starts on the platform (Stage 1).

1960–62
Utzon resolves the dilemma of the roof's design and construction in 1961. Sir Eugene Goosens dies in 1962.

1963–65
Work starts on the roof (Stage 2). In 1965 a Liberal/Country Party Coalition elected to office promises to stem rising costs and construction delays.

1966
On 28 February, Utzon resigns after disputes with the government over designs, deadlines, fees, subcontractors, and his role as the architect. A 1,000 people march on state Parliament demanding his reinstatement. Four Australian architects are appointed to complete the project. Utzon leaves Australia.

1966–1973
The Northern Foyers, interiors, walkways and concourse are completed (Stage 3).

1973
At the Forecourt on 20 October 1973, Queen Elizabeth II formally declares the Sydney Opera House open. Final cost: $102 million. Final project duration: 14 years.

The Red Book, *submitted for the 1957 design competition, contains Utzon's original sketches for the Opera House.*

Top 10 "Performances"

1. 1960: Paul Robeson performs for construction workers.
2. 1973: A possum appears at a dress rehearsal for the House's first production.
3. 1975: Shostakovich conducts his father's Symphony Number 10 only days after his father's death.
4. 1983: Joan Sutherland and Luciano Pavarotti perform the "Concert of the Century"
5. 1986: Pope John Paul II addresses religious orders in the Hall.
6. 1990: Nelson Mandela gives a public address.
7. 1990: Joan Sutherland takes her final bow.
8. 1992: Peter Allen performs for the last time.
9. 2003: Protesters daub "No War" on the roof in protest at Australia's involvement in Iraq.
10. 2006: Queen Elizabeth II opens the Colonnade, the first exterior change to the building.

Designing the House

Jørn Utzon

Inspired by the fan-like ribs of a palm leaf, Utzon's intention was to construct a timeless, organic structure with an ascetic exterior that defied conventional expectations of function and significance. The shells were to float above the harbour like giant sails. Utzon's drawings were inspired, but didn't allow for cost-effective prefabrication. In partnership with the engineering firm Ove Arup & Partners, Utzon laboured for months over the issue. His elegant epiphany came in 1961. If the shells were all cast from the same sphere, thus sharing a radius, it would be possible to pre-cast the concrete ribs as segments which could then be later assembled. After the plan's viability was confirmed, work on the roof began in 1963. In 2003, Utzon's genius was recognised by the architecture world's equivalent of the Nobel Prize, the Pritzker Prize.

Segmented globe   Roof comes into view

Utzon's Opera House Model

Utzon's original interiors and certain design features now only exist in model form. The architect donated his models and plans to the State Library of New South Wales (see p22).

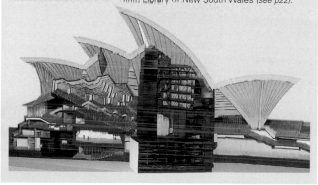

🔟 Sydney Harbour Bridge

Nothing you've ever seen can prepare you for the size and surprising beauty of the world's largest steel arch bridge, opened in 1932. Its balanced composition and the graceful sweep of its southern approach have captivated artists for years. Francis Greenway (see p23) proposed a bridge in 1815, but the logistics vexed engineers until 1911, when John Bradfield suggested a single-span bridge. By then North Shore's rapid growth demanded a solution, the only alternative being a long road trip through the western suburbs. Most visitors can easily understand why Sydneysiders love their old "coathanger".

The Harbour Bridge

🍸 Enjoy a cocktail on the rooftop of the Harbour View Hotel, where you'll be almost level with returning bridge climbers.

🏊 For a unique perspective on the bridge, lounge at the North Sydney Olympic Pool beneath the bridge.

- Map D2
- BridgeClimb: 5 Cumberland St, The Rocks; 8274 7777; www.bridgeclimb.com; operates daily; adult/ child (minimun age: 10) $179–$295/$109–$195 (prices rise in peak season: 26 Dec–9 Jan)
- Southeast Pylon Lookout: 9240 1100; www.pylonlookout.com. au; open 10am–5pm daily; closed 25 Dec; adult/ children 8–12 $9.50/$4
- Harbour View Hotel: Cumberland St, The Rocks; www.harbour view.com.au
- Pedestrian path entry: Cumberland St, The Rocks; Cycle path entry: Observatory Park

Top 10 Features

1. Design
2. BridgeClimb
3. Pylon Lookout & Museum
4. Pedestrian & Cycle Paths
5. Bradfield Park
6. Dawes Point
7. Maintenance
8. Tolls
9. Famous Portraits
10. Memorial

1 Design

Engineer John Bradfield established the design parameters, completed by Dorman Long & Co. Sir John Burnet and Partners of London designed the decorative granite-clad Art Deco pylons.

2 BridgeClimb

Since BridgeClimb *(above)* opened for business in 1998, almost two million people have climbed the bridge. The 3.5-hour guided climb is well organised and exhilarating, and there's no better way to appreciate the structure's enormity and beauty.

Poster for the Bridge's opening

3 Pylon Lookout & Museum

The Southeast Pylon *(below)* offers 360-degree spectacular bridge-top views of Sydney as well as three levels of exhibition space exploring the bridge's genesis.

4 Pedestrian & Cycle Paths

Free highlights include a pedestrian and jogging path *(above)* along the eastern side of the bridge, and a cycle path along the western side.

6 Dawes Point

Below the southern pylons is Dawes Point, where the colony's first observatory was built in 1788. The park's interpretation boards, and the excavated remains of the fort that replaced the observatory in 1791, offer an interesting perspective on the city's development.

9 Famous Portraits

Works by renowned artists such as Grace Cossington-Smith, Dorrit Black, Gwen Barringer and Henri Mallard reflect the optimism inspired by the bridge in the midst of the Great Depression, and honour the bravery of its construction workers.

10 Memorial

During the Great Depression 1,400 people *(above)* worked on the bridge while hundreds more worked for subcontractors. A plaque on the southern approach commemorates the 16 workers who lost their lives during construction.

5 Bradfield Park

Under the northern pylons, this small park commemorating John Bradfield offers unparalleled views of the Opera House and Circular Quay. Directly beneath the bridge is the bow of the original HMAS *Sydney*.

7 Maintenance

Over $14 million and 3000 litres of paint a year are needed to keep the bridge shipshape. Before establishing himself as an actor, Paul Hogan worked as a painter on the bridge.

8 Tolls

When the bridge opened in 1932, the toll for cars was 6 pence. Horse and carts cost 3 pence and sheep and pigs were a penny per head. The current toll for vehicles *(left)* is $3.

"Captain" Francis de Groot

Before Premier JT Lang could cut the ceremonial ribbon at the bridge's 1932 opening, a man swept forward and slashed the ribbon. "Captain" Francis de Groot declared the bridge open in the name of "decent citizens of NSW". He belonged to the right-wing New Guard, which opposed Lang's "socialist" government and believed that only royalty should inaugurate such an achievement. He was arrested and sent to a psychiatric hospital while Lang re-cut the ribbon.

Paul Hogan's big break was the starring role in the hugely popular movie Crocodile Dundee *(1986).*

Sydney Harbour

Arguably the most beautiful harbour in the world, it took the Parramatta and Lane Cove Rivers thousands of years to carve it from the sandstone. Well protected from off-shore winds, the harbour is also remarkably deep in parts. From its working docklands to its pristine and secluded beaches, this harbour is a natural asset that most cities can only dream of. Over the last 200 years the harbour has seen vast real estate developments, now comprising a lively array of apartment buildings and large residences, each vying for vantage points of the gorgeous harbour views and bustling maritime life.

A harbour beacon

🛒 Pack a picnic hamper and catch a water taxi to Clark Island for an al fresco lunch. There are picnic tables along the foreshore and walking trails through the bushland. Contact NPWS for details.

☀ On a sunny day, carry your bathing gear and towel on a harbourside walk. You will surely stumble upon an inviting beach or a harbourside pool.

• Map E2
• NSW/NPWS Information line: 1300 361 967
• Sydney Harbour Tours: Cadmans Cottage, 110 George St, The Rocks; 9247 5033; Open 9:30am–4:30pm Mon–Fri, 10am–4:30pm Sat–Sun; Closed Good Friday, 25 Dec
• Sydney Harbour Federation Trust: 8969 2100 • www. harbourtrust.gov.au

Top 10 Attractions

1. Sydney Harbour National Park
2. Harbour Beaches
3. The Heads
4. The Islands
5. Harbourside Walks
6. Harbourside Mansions & Penthouses
7. Harbourside Parks
8. Harbour Wildlife
9. The Working Harbour
10. Ferry Rides

1 Sydney Harbour National Park

This remarkable national park includes 5 islands. Aboriginal rock art sites, historic buildings, secluded beaches, monuments, lookouts and bushwalks are just some of its highlights. The National Parks and Wildlife Service (NPWS) manages the park and operates several tours.

2 Harbour Beaches

Sydney's harbour beaches *(below)* are glorious and several have protective shark netting, including Shark Beach and Manly Cove *(see p118)*. Parsley Bay, Camp Cove, and Lady Bay Beach in Watsons Bay are all gems and are accessible by ferry.

Aerial view of the harbour

3 The Heads

The rugged South and North Heads *(above & p51)* mark the entrance to Sydney Harbour and offer magnificent ocean and harbour views. They are particularly popular on Boxing Day when crowds gather to cheer on the Sydney to Hobart yacht race *(see p73)*.

Sign up for DK's email newsletter on traveldk.com

4 The Islands
Of the harbour's seven islands, Sydney Harbour Federation Trust manages Cockatoo and Snapper, and the NPWS manages Goat, Shark, Clark, Rodd Fort Denison *(above)*.

6 Harbourside Mansions & Penthouses
Among the fabulous abodes are Boomerang *(see p86)*, built by music publisher Frank Albert, Craigend (Darling Point, owned by shipping magnate James Patrick), and Russell Crowe's penthouse at Woolloomooloo Finger Wharf *(see p86)*.

9 The Working Harbour
View the harbour's working history at the Australian National Maritime Museum *(see p42)*, wander Balmain's backstreets, or discover the convict and maritime history of Cockatoo Island with the Sydney Harbour Federation Trust.

10 Ferry Rides
No trip to Sydney is complete without a ferry ride *(above & pp16–17)*. A journey to Manly is the classic trip, but other popular destinations include Watsons Bay, Balmain, Mosman and Darling Harbour.

5 Harbourside Walks
Thanks to the Harbour Foreshore Vigilance Committee *(see p97)*, set up to retain harbourside land for public use, Sydney has great harbourside walks. Sydney ferries' *Go Walkabout* booklet is a pocket-sized guide to some of the best options.

7 Harbourside Parks
While some parks offer extensive walking trails, others are lovely pockets of shaded greenery. The best parks include Rushcutters Bay *(see p87)*, Balls Head Reserve *(see p115)*, the Botanic Gardens *(see pp20–21)* and Nielson Park *(see p51)*.

8 Harbour Wildlife
Sydney Harbour is remarkably healthy, home to rainbow lorikeets *(left)*, several species of shark and fish, sea horses, dolphins, the occasional whale and the only known Little Penguin breeding colony on the Australian mainland.

HMAS Kuttabul
Three Japanese midget submarines passed through Sydney Heads on 31 May 1942. One sub aimed at the US naval ship *Chicago* but its torpedo missed and sank a Sydney ferry serving as a dormitory ship for Australian and British soldiers, the HMAS *Kuttabul*. The *Kuttabul* sank within minutes and 21 soldiers died. A chase ensued: one sub escaped, one was sunk by depth charges, and one set off its own charges and sank. Two subs were recovered and their four crew members were buried with full military honours.

Left **State ferry** Centre **Water taxi** Right **Seaplane**

10 On the Water

1 Ferries
It's been over 135 years since the first row boats transported customers across the harbour. Now 31 ferries offer eight fantastic routes.

2 Jet & River Cats
If you plan to visit Sydney Olympic Park or Parramatta's historic attractions, avoid the congestion of Parramatta Road by taking one of the sleek River Cat Ferries. If you can't wait for a swim at Manly Beach, catch the Jet Cat.

3 Spectator Ferry
Catch a spectator ferry which follows the famous 18 Footers Skiff racing on the harbour on weekends.
www.18footers.com.au

4 Water Taxis
Although too expensive for daily commuting, these taxis are a fun option if you fancy a peek at the luxurious harbourside mansions or a picnic on one of the islands.

Boats of all sizes at Circular Quay

5 Catamarans
Several gigantic catamarans service the harbour tourist trade. In some cases you can enjoy an on-board BBQ, or work on your tan as you cruise the harbour.

6 Jet Boats
If you feel the urge to "burn rubber" on the harbour, the harbour's jet boats will definitely give you an adrenaline fix.

7 Tall Ships
If they're in town, enjoy a harbour voyage on either of Sydney's two tall ships, the *Svanen* or the *Bounty*, a replica of Bligh's vessel built for the film of the same name.

8 Boats for Hire
Rent anything from sea kayaks to 14-ft (4.3-m) aluminium boats to 20-ft (6-m) half-cabin cruisers. Or hire a kayak and explore Middle Harbour.

9 Seaplane
Numerous flights around Sydney Harbour offer excellent fly-and-dine packages and can also take you to the gorgeous Northern Beaches, Pittwater and Hawkesbury regions.

10 Helicopter
For a touch of *Mission Impossible*, catch a helicopter for an exciting and scenic ride over the Harbour Bridge, the Opera House, Eastern Suburbs and Manly Cove.

Top 10 Famous Harbourside Residents

1. John Howard, former Prime Minister
2. John Laws, radio shock-jock
3. Craig Parry, golfer
4. Judy Davis & Colin Friels, actors
5. Ken Done, artist
6. Jimmy Barnes, singer
7. May Gibbs, author
8. Nicole Kidman, actor
9. Cate Blanchett, actor
10. Russell Crowe, actor

• Jet & River Cats depart from Circular Quay • Morning cruise: 1 hr, adult/child $18/$9; Afternoon cruise: 2.5 hrs, adult/child $24/$12; Evening cruise: 1.5 hrs, adult/child $22/$11 • Jet Boats: Sydney Jet & Oz Jet Boating www.sydneyjet.com, www.ozjetboating.com
• Kayak: Sydney Harbour Kayaks under the Spit Bridge in Mosman • Boats, yachts & cruisers: Sydney Harbour Escapes, Rose Bay (see p55)
• Seaplane companies: Rose Bay • Sydney Heli Tours: Mascot, SydneyAirport
• Sydney Ferries: www.sydneyferries.info

Sailing on Sydney Harbour

Sydney Harbour is perfect for sailing, although sometimes you can't see the water for the canvas. Wednesday afternoons and weekends are popular with the more competitive old salts, especially in the the competition season which runs between September and March. Friday twilight sailing is perfect for the more laid-back yachtie. Several firms, including Sydney Harbour Escapes, hire yachts for bareboat charter and offer social sailing and sailing lessons on Fridays and Sundays. The Sailing School, Sydney by Sail, and East Sail can also teach you the ropes. Afloat is a free monthly magazine for the yachting fraternity and for those with an interest in Sydney's maritime history. It also carries a regular calendar of events, tide charts and fishing tips. Check the Crew Wanted classifieds if you fancy running away to sea; Afloat is available at all marinas and the Australian National Maritime Museum.

Sydney to Hobart Yacht Race

Sailing on the harbour

🔟 The Rocks & Circular Quay

Near Circular Quay, The Rocks is a sanitized precinct of narrow laneways, galleries, boutiques and restaurants. West of the Argyle Cut, the road cut through solid rock in the 1860s that links east with west, the area is mainly residential. The Rocks sprang up beside the Tank Stream following the First Fleet's arrival on 26 January 1788. Within days, Governor Phillip's prefabricated canvas and timber residence was erected and the convicts housed in tents beneath the sandstone outcrops that gave The Rocks its name. Nowadays the open sewers, drunken sailors, convicts, brothels and plague-ridden rats are long gone, and the area is ideal for a winding stroll and a cold ale at a historic hotel; try the Hero of Waterloo or the Lord Nelson.

The Hero of Waterloo pub

🍺 **The Australian Hotel at Cumberland and Gloucester Streets serves great pizzas.**

🍺 **To meet the locals, have a drink at the Mercantile Hotel on George Street.**

- Map M1
- Sailors' Home:Billich Gallery, 106 George St; 9255 1788; Open 9:30am–5pm daily
- Cadmans Cottage: 110 George St; Open 10am–4:30pm Mon–Fri, 10:30am–4:30pm Sat–Sun
- Garrison Church: Argyle & Lower Fort Sts; Open 9am–5pm daily
- Sydney Observatory: Watson Rd; 9921 3485; Open 10am–5pm daily; General entry free, Adm for theatre & planetarium
- Hero of Waterloo: 81 Lower Fort St
- Lord Nelson Hotel: see p146

Top 10 Features

1. Circular Quay
2. Customs House
3. Tank Stream
4. George Street
5. Sailors' Home
6. Cadmans Cottage
7. Museum of Contemporary Art
8. Overseas Passenger Terminal
9. Garrison Church
10. Sydney Observatory

Circular Quay
This maritime hub is Sydney's nucleus. Plaques in the paving record observations about Australia by authors such as Mark Twain, Umberto Eco and Germaine Greer.

Customs House
Recent renovations of this stately 1844 building saw the addition of a major new public library. The Union Jack on Loftus Street marks the site of European landing and settlement.

Tank Stream
The only harbourfront reminders of the tidal creek *(see p38)* that determined Sydney's location are two artworks on Alfred Street. Stephen Walker's is at the western end, and Lynne Roberts-Goodwin's *(see p47)* is at the corner of Pitt Street.

George Street
Australia's oldest street is now a busy stretch of boutiques, galleries, shops and pubs. The Rocks' market below) selling crafts, jewellery and the like is held at the northern end of the street on Saturdays and Sundays from 10am–5pm.

5 Sailors' Home
Formed in 1859, the Sailors' Home ran until the 1970s providing cheap lodging to seamen. Home to the Billich Gallery, the building's original north wing is Romanesque Revival in design.

6 Cadmans Cottage
Built in 1816, this is Sydney's oldest surviving dwelling *(right)*. It contains items excavated beneath the floors and the National Park Information Centre.

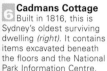

10 Sydney Observatory
The 1858 Italianate building *(below)* was converted into a museum of astronomy in 1988. The tower's time-ball still drops daily at 1 pm, while a cannon is fired simultaneously from Fort Denison *(see p38)*.

7 Museum of Contemporary Art
The cutting-edge MCA displays contemporary art from Australia and around the world *(above & p44)*. Its guided tours, free exhibitions and lectures by artists and curators are always well attended.

8 Overseas Passenger Terminal
A stylish glass structure containing excellent restaurants, its 1988 renovation replaced the 1950s terminal that once accommodated passenger liners. Its views of the Opera House are unparalleled.

9 Garrison Church
Australia's first military church is officially named Holy Trinity Church *(below)*. Designed by Henry Ginn in 1840, it was remodelled in 1878 by Edmund Blacket, Colonial architect of the Victorian Gothic main building at Sydney University *(see p103)*.

Lieutenant William Dawes
Lieutenant Dawes established Australia's first observatory on the point that now bears his name. In 1790 he earned Governor Phillip's displeasure when he refused to join a reprisal attack against Aborigines. His refusal sprang from his relationship with a Eora woman, Patyegarang. Dawes' journals detail his conversations with Patyegarang and document the vocabulary and grammar of the Eora. Dawes was shipped out in 1791 and spent years campaigning against slavery in the West Indies.

🔟 Royal Botanic Gardens & The Domain

Located around Farm Cove on the shore of Sydney Harbour is the spectacular Royal Botanic Gardens and Domain. Established in 1816, this oasis in the heart of the city occupies the land on which the first crops were planted. Australia's oldest scientific institution is home to an impressive collection of native and exotic plants and trees. The grounds also house an art gallery and music school.

Water lily at the gardens

🍴 **The Poolside Café at the "Boy" Charlton Pool has baguettes and light lunches.**

🎬 **During the Sydney Festival, the Open Air Cinema makes for a a lovely evening.**

• Map N3
• Royal Botanic Gardens: Mrs Macquarie's Rd; open 7am–sunset daily; www.rbgsyd.nsw.gov.au
• Visitor Information Centre: 9231 8125 ; Open 9:30am–4:30pm daily • Andrew "Boy" Charlton Pool: Mrs Macquarie's Rd; 9358 6686; Open 6am–7pm daily; adult/child $5.50/$3.80
• Sydney Tropical Centre: 9231 8104; Open 10am–4pm daily; Adm
• Conservatorium of Music: 9351 1222; Open 9am–5pm Mon–Fri, 9am–4pm Sat
• Government House: 9931 5222; House open 10:30am–3pm Fri–Sun (Tours every half hour from 10:30am), Grounds open 10am–4pm daily

Top 10 Attractions

1. Mrs Macquarie's Chair
2. Andrew "Boy" Charlton Pool
3. Wollemi Pine
4. Cadi Jam Ora: First Encounters
5. Palm House
6. Art Gallery of New South Wales
7. Sydney Tropical Centre
8. Conservatorium of Music
9. Government House
10. Walks & Tours

1 Mrs Macquarie's Chair
This sandstone bench *(above)* was carved in 1816 for the governor's wife, Elizabeth Macquarie. The landmark offers breath-taking views of the Opera House, Harbour Bridge and Fort Denison.

2 Andrew "Boy" Charlton Pool
Named for a 16-year-old Olympic winner, this glorious 50m (164-ft) pool overlooks Woolloomooloo Bay and Garden Island. Its patrons take their laps and suntans seriously, but the toddlers' pool is perfect for those who just want to dip their toes.

The lush Royal Botanic Gardens

3 Wollemi Pine
Discovered in 1994 in a Blue Mountains *(below & p121)* canyon, this botanical curiosity was thought to be extinct. The Royal Botanic Garden's specimen was planted in 1998.

During the Sydney Festival, call 1300 366 649 for details of the Open Air Cinema.

Cadi Jam Ora: First Encounters

This award-winning presentation of the Eora people's story offers an intriguing look at white settlement, Sydney's environment, and the Eora's spiritual connection with their land.

Sydney Tropical Centre

Tropical ecosystems are recreated in the centre's two glasshouses *(above)*, the Pyramid and the Arc. The Pyramid features Australian natives, while the Arc houses the "exotics". Follow the walkways up to the canopy level to admire plants from the tropics.

Conservatorium of Music

Designed by Francis Greenway *(see p23)*, this building *(below)* was one of the first casualties of the enquiry into the cost of Macquarie's public works. "The Con" has been training future musicians since 1915.

Palm House

The Victorian era glass house was designed by James Barnet *(see p77)* to display tropical plants. The plants are now in the Sydney Tropical Centre and the Palm House is used for art exhibitions.

Art Gallery of New South Wales

The AGNSW *(right & pp24–25)* has a permanent collection of Australian, European, Asian and indigenous art.

Walks & Tours

The Royal Botanic Garden's volunteers conduct free guided walks which depart from the Garden's shop. The walks run daily at 10:30am and also at 1pm on weekdays during autumn, winter and spring except for public holidays. An Aboriginal Heritage Tour is conducted every Friday at 2pm and costs $25 per person.

Government House

Gipps was the first governor to occupy this Gothic Revival structure in 1845. It ceased to be the governor's residence in 1996, and the house and grounds are now open to the public.

Mrs Biggs' Bathing Box

The Eora enjoyed the sheltered waters of Woolloomooloo Bay for thousands of years before young Andrew Charlton won the 1,500-m (1,640-yard) race at the 1924 Olympics. The colony's first public baths, The Fig Tree Baths, stood on the site of the "Boy" Charlton pool. Several establishments once catered to the delicate sensibilities of Sydney's lady bathers, including one owned by a Mrs Biggs. An artwork by Robyn Backen, *The Archaeology of Bathing*, recalls Mrs Biggs' 1833 Bathing Machine, designed to protect the modesty of her patrons from bothersome manly gazes as well as sharks.

Left **Parliament House** Centre **Entrance of Sydney Hospital** Right **Mural at St James Church**

🔟 Macquarie Street Precinct

1 The Astor
One of Sydney's first skyscrapers, this elegant 1920s apartment building has housed artistic notables such as artist Portia Geach and actor, writer and comic Barry Humphries.

2 State Library of NSW
More than five million items are held in the Library's Mitchell (1910) and Macquarie (1988) Wings (see p45). The exhibition spaces showcase this collection and the library holds a range of talks and events. Free tours are run on Tuesdays and Thursdays.

3 Parliament House
The oldest parliament house in the world began in 1816 as a wing of the "Rum Hospital", built by contractors licensed to import rum into the colony in lieu of payment. The New South Wales Legislative Council held its first meeting here in 1829.

4 Sydney Hospital
This structure replaced the central wing of the Rum Hospital in the 1880s. The statue of a boar, *Il Porcellino*, is a replica of a 1547 Florentine artwork.

5 Martin Place
Australia's grandest banks reside on this broad plaza (see p77). A Cenotaph near George Street commemorates Australia's war dead, and *The Passage* by Anne Graham celebrates Sydney's Georgian heritage.

6 Mint Museum
An elegant museum and home to the Historic Houses Trust, this 1816 Rum Hospital wing was converted in 1854 into a branch of London's Royal Mint. ◐ Open 9:30am–5pm Mon–Fri

7 Hyde Park Barracks
Perhaps Francis Greenway's finest work, these barracks were built in 1819 to house convicts. Later a hostel for immigrant women and then courtrooms, since 1979 it has been a museum of the site and its varied occupants (see p42).

8 Great Irish Famine Memorial
Built into a barrack wall is this memorial to the victims of the Famine (1845–48). This catastrophe forced 30,000 Irish women and over 4,000 orphans to migrate to Australia; some were housed at the barracks.

9 St James Church
Another Greenway gem, this 1822 church was originally intended as a court house. Don't miss the superb 1930s mural in the Children's Chapel.

10 Queen's Square
Governor Macquarie envisaged this small square as Sydney's civic centre. In the 1890s it was a rallying point for protesters, among them Republicans who would mount Queen Victoria's statue to address the masses.

Top 10 Convicts Made Good

1. Francis Greenway (1777–1837), forger to government architect
2. William "Billy" Blue (1734–1834), sugar thief to pioneer ferryman
3. Simeon Lord (1771–1840), fabric thief to merchant, magistrate
4. William Redfern (1774–1833), naval mutineer to surgeon
5. Mary Reiley (1777–1855), horse thief to entrepreneur
6. Henry Kable (1763–1846), burglar to merchant
7. George Howe (1769–1821), shoplifter to publisher
8. Edward Eagar (1787–1866), forger to lawyer
9. George Crossley (1749–1823), perjurer to lawyer
10. Samuel Terry (1776–1838), stocking thief to publican, landowner and moneylender

Inside the barracks

Replica convict hammocks stretch across the third floor of the barracks.

Francis Greenway: Convict Architect

Detail of Hyde Park Barracks wall

Inspired. Vain. Delusional. No single epithet adequately describes Francis Howard Greenway. In 1809 Greenway, a partner in an architectural firm, was found guilty of forging a contract, and was sentenced to 14 years in the colony. Soon after his arrival in 1814, Governor Macquarie realised that Greenway's architectural talent was equal to his own Enlightenment aspirations, and in 1816 he appointed Greenway as Colonial Architect and Assistant Engineer. Starting with the Macquarie Lighthouse on South Head, Greenway and Governor and Mrs Macquarie set about transforming Sydney's civic landscape. Unfortunately, not everyone shared their ambitions, and reports of extravagance filtered back to London. Commissioner JT Bigge arrived in Sydney in 1819 to investigate and halted most public works. His censure of the Macquaries' taste for ornamentation deprived Greenway of his patrons, who departed the colony in 1822. Despite his major contribution to the standard of Colonial architecture, Greenway struggled in private practice and died a poor man in 1837.

Hyde Park Barracks

The Historic Houses Trust run tours of Hyde Park Barracks and the Mint Museum; call 8239 2311 for details.

TO 10 Art Gallery of New South Wales

Conceived in the 1870s and opened to the public in 1909, AGNSW contains some of the finest artworks in Australia. Situated on a grand drive in The Domain, it has always been a wonderful place to escape the heat and bustle of the city. The gallery has been extended several times in the last four decades and houses a significant collection of Australian, Asian and European art. There are approximately 40 temporary exhibitions per year, and the permanent collection rotates quarterly.

Entrance to AGNSW

🞂 Re-energise your tired eyes and feet with a snack at the AGNSW café.

🞂 The AGNSW shop stocks exhibition catalogues, gifts, postcards, unusual souvenirs and a huge range of art books.

Sundays are Fundays for kids, with art shows on various topics. There are also frequent classes and workshops.

• Map N3
• Art Gallery Rd, The Domain
• 9225 1744
• www.artgallery.nsw.gov.au
• See works on paper that are not on display in the Study Room. It's best to make a booking 9225 1758

Top 10 Attractions

1. Exterior
2. Southern Galleries
3. Yiribana Gallery
4. New Asian Galleries
5. Australian Art Collection
6. Photography Collection
7. Temporary Exhibitions
8. Art After Hours
9. Archibald, Wynne & Sulman Prizes
10. Café & Restaurant

1 Exterior
Walter Liberty Vernon designed the striking colonnaded entrance and ornamented walls of this stucture in the Classical style *(below)*.

2 Southern Galleries
These rooms contain the oldest works at AGNSW, for the largely British art *(below)* displayed here was initially the gallery's focus. The lovely rooms complement the many noteworthy works.

3 Yiribana Gallery
Dedicated to Aboriginal art and culture, the works here range from bark paintings and traditional designs on canvas to works by contemporary Aboriginal artists such as Lin Onus.

4 New Asian Galleries
Lit up like a Chinese lantern at night, this 2003 gallery highlights the different traditions, periods and cultures of Asia. The artworks *(right)* are accompanied by fact cards providing historical and cultural backgrounds.

5 Australian Art Collection
Featuring major names in Australian art, this collection displays works by luminaries such as Sidney Nolan, Grace Cossington-Smith *(left)*, Brett Whiteley and Arthur Boyd. There are many works by local Sydney artists *(see p26)* and several great images of the city.

6 Photography Collection
From Muybridge's first experimentation with photographs to artists such as Cindy Sherman, Tracey Moffat and Hans Hasenpflug *(below)*, the world's most significant names in photography are well represented here.

Key

	Lower Level 1
	Ground Level
	Lower Level 2
	Lower Level 3

7 Temporary Exhibitions
Several spaces at AGNSW are dedicated to temporary exhibitions. While some display contemporary art, others are retrospectives spanning a movement or an artist's career. Entry can entail a minor fee.

8 Art After Hours
On Wednesday nights until 9pm, the gallery draws a keen after-work crowd with its free film screenings, celebrity talks, jazz and access to all exhibitions.

9 Archibald, Wynne & Sulman Prizes
The annual Archibald prize is for portraiture, the Sulman for genre painting and the Wynne for landscape painting

Looking Towards Asia
AGNSW's collection of Asian art began in 1879, when the Japanese Government made a large donation of ceramics and bronzes. However, it didn't become a distinct department until 1979, when Edmund Capon was appointed gallery director. Capon wisely noted that the art of Asia is the art of half of the world. With him at the helm, the AGNSW has extended the collection to include Southeast Asian textiles, Buddhist arts, Japanese Screens, Indian sculptures and Ming, Qing and modern Chinese paintings.

10 Café & Restaurant
The AGNSW café is a great spot to take a break. It serves good coffee, lunch and snacks, as well as wine and beer, and has a gorgeous view of the harbour and Woolloomooloo. The swish restaurant has a similar view and an extensive menu.

Catch the train to Martin Place and walk through the grounds of Sydney Hospital and across the Domain.

Left **Brett Whiteley** Centre **John Olsen** Right **Detail from Grace Cossington-Smith's** *Self Portrait*

Top 10 Sydney Artists

1 Brett Whiteley (1939–92)
The bad boy of Australian art, Whiteley *(see p93)* was a prodigious talent who won the trifecta of Archibald, Wynne and Sulman prizes *(see p25)* twice in consecutive years. He died of a heroin overdose in 1992.

2 John Olsen (b. 1928)
Considered Australia's most esteemed living painter, Olsen was awarded the Order of Australia in 2001. Olsen has travelled widely in Australia and abroad, continuously mapping his travels with paintings.

3 Lloyd Rees (1895–1988)
Renowned for his landscape paintings, Rees also produced hundreds of drawings, many of which are in the collection of AGNSW. He began printmaking in his 80s, and continued to etch even while losing his sight.

4 Grace Cossington-Smith (1892–1984)
Sydney's first significant female artist, she was particularly interested in form and colour. She painted still lifes, landscapes and religious subjects.

5 Max Dupain (1911–92)
Dupain recorded much of Australia's architectural history through his art, both Colonial and Modern. However, it is for his wonderful iconoclastic 1937 photo, *The Sunbaker*, that he is most celebrated.

6 Margaret Olley (b. 1923)
Olley has always concentrated on painting still lifes and interiors. In 1948 William Dobell won the Archibald for his portrait of Olley, which is in the AGNSW's collection.

7 Margaret Preston (1875–1963)
Preston's art was highly influenced by Pacific Islander, Chinese and Japanese cultures. Recognising the value of Aboriginal art, she was a key figure in the Australian Modernist movement.

8 William Yang (b. 1943)
Initially a playwright, he moved into social photography and documented Sydney's blossoming gay community, bringing it from the underworld into the spotlight.

9 Susan Norrie (b. 1953)
One of Australia's most successful contemporary artists, Norrie works in multiple media. Her works are displayed in the collections of significant galleries such as the Guggenheim and the MCA *(see p44)*.

10 Imants Tillers (b. 1950)
A former architect, he designed the roof of the Federation Pavilion in Centennial Park *(see pp39 & 47)*. Interestingly, Tillers works on small canvas boards simply because they fit on his drawing board.

Images of Sydney

Since the first Europeans arrived in the late 18th century, artists have been documenting the changing landscape of Sydney. In early years, Sydney was often painted as a kind of fantasy, using the familiar green slopes of England instead of the new dry, strange land. Eventually Sydney's settlers stopped wishing for the pastures left behind, and subsequent generations rejoiced in the blue skies and sparkling harbour. The construction of the Harbour Bridge inspired a whole new group of artists, who photographed as well as painted it, signalling the emergence of Sydney as an international city. Brett Whiteley concocted luscious images of the harbour and its surrounds in the 1970s, and in the 1980s Ken Done made his fortune selling clothes printed with bright sketches of the Opera House. Now more than ever, Sydney artists are part of the global artistic community.

Eugene Von Guérard, *Sydney Heads*, 1865

Brett Whiteley, *The Balcony 2*, 1975
This powerful oil on canvas can be found at the AGNSW, where it has been exhibited since 1981. Brett Whiteley produced some of the most distinctive and vivid images of Sydney and its harbour ever painted.

⑩ Darling Harbour & Chinatown

Cockle Bay was once a working harbour district where some of Sydney's poorest lived in hovels surrounded by shipyards, cargo wharves and quarries. In anticipation of the 1988 Bicentenary, a huge redevelopment project was launched to reclaim this 54-ha (133-acre) site, and the area was revitalised through the wonderful Aquarium, the Maritime and Powerhouse Museums, and the Cockle Bay and King St. Wharf developments. Combined with a visit to Chinatown, Darling Harbour makes for a lively and entertaining excursion.

Endeavour replica

🍰 Pop into Maxim's Cakes for something delicious; Goulburn and Sussex Streets.

• *Map L5*
• *Sydney Aquarium: Aquarium Pier, Darling Harbour; 8251 7800; Open 9am–10pm daily; www.sydneyaquarium. com.au; adult/child $29.95/$15*
• *Chinese Garden: Darling Harbour; 9240 8888; Open 9:30am– 5pm daily, closed Good Fri & 25 Dec; www. chinesegarden.com.au; adult/child $6/$3*
• *Capitol Theatre: 13 Campbell St, Haymarket; 9320 5000; www. capitoltheatre.com.au*
• *Paddy's Market: Hay and Thomas Sts, Haymarket; 1300 361 589; Open 9am–5pm Thu– Sun & public holiday Mon*
• *Market City: Paddy's Market; 9212 1388; Open 10am–7pm daily except 10am–8pm Thu*
• *Sydney Wildlife World: Aquarium Pier, Darling Harbour; 9333 9288; Open 9am–6pm daily; www.sydneywildlife world.com.au; adult/child $29.95/$15*

Top 10 Attractions

1. Australian National Maritime Museum
2. Pyrmont Bridge
3. Cockle Bay & King St. Wharves
4. Sydney Aquarium
5. Chinese Garden
6. Chinatown
7. Capitol Theatre
8. Paddy's Market
9. Powerhouse Museum
10. Sydney Wildlife World

① Australian National Maritime Museum

At this exploration of Australia's relationship with the sea, visitors can climb aboard vessels, or view exhibits dealing with immigration, maritime archaeology, beach culture and more *(above & p42)*.

② Pyrmont Bridge

Opened in 1902, this 369-m (1,210-ft) bridge, with a quaint copper-roofed control cabin, is the oldest electrically-operated swingspan bridge in the world. It swings open to allow vessels up to 14 m (46ft) tall to enter or depart Cockle Bay.

③ Cockle Bay & King St. Wharves

King St. Wharf is a social mecca for the working crowd. Cockle Bay *(above)* comprises a three-storey hive of cafés, restaurants, bars and function centres.

④ Sydney Aquarium

See over 12,000 all-Australian aquatic animals, including sharks, rays and crocodiles. Ride the new glass-bottomed boat over tropical fish in Australia's largest Great Barrier Reef display *(below)*.

Chinese Garden
5 China's gift to Sydney is one of only a handful of traditional gardens outside China *(left)*. Interpretation boards provide insights into Chinese garden design and philosophy, and the Tea House makes for a peaceful retreat from the harbour.

Sydney Wildlife World
10 Next door to Sydney Aquarium, visit over 100 Australian native animals in their natural habitats. There are various tours available which provide interactive experiences with the animals *(below)*.

Chinatown
6 This is the spirited epicentre of Sydney's very large Chinese community, where restaurants vie for attention with fabric shops, Asian grocers, jewellers, music stores and gift shops. It is best visited for a Friday night market. Chinese New Year celebrations here (Jan/Feb) are among the largest and most spectacular outside Asia.

Capitol Theatre
7 Built in the 1920s, this theatre has seen many comebacks. Its most recent restoration in the 1990s gave the Mediterranean-blue ceiling and twinkling stars a new lease on life. The orchestra pit at Capitol is the largest in the country. It is now a well-known venue for popular musicals.

Paddy's Market
8 Associated with the Haymarket area for 150 years, Paddy's Market is the place to find a pair of koala oven mitts or an Opera House watch, as well as food *(below)*, souvenirs, flowers, homeware and cheap accessories. Market City has clothing outlets and entertainment venues.

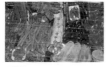

Powerhouse Museum
9 At Australia's most inventive and engaging museum, children are not the only ones to enjoy the interactive displays. A child-friendly café is located on the lowest gallery level of the museum *(see pp30–31)*.

"Buffalo Bill" Cole's Wild West Show
In the early 1900s, the intersection opposite Paddy's Market was a regular venue for "Buffalo Bill" Cole's Wild West Show. The English-born owner of the circus, Edward Cole, and his American partner, "Texas Jack", recruited a cast of locals to dress as cowboys and Indians and enact a wagon train ambush on horseback. Cole, as Buffalo Bill, always rode to the rescue of the besieged pioneers. In later years Cole modified his performance and included Australia's most famous bushranger, Ned Kelly, in the show's line-up.

 Enjoy a leisurely yum cha at one of Chinatown's many excellent restaurants (see p82).

29

ⓉⓄⓅ10 Powerhouse Museum

One of Sydney's most distinguished and popular cultural institutions, the museum's extensive science and design collection is thought-provoking, quirky and interactive. You could sit in an electric chair, match wits with an encryption machine, or play catch-up with an industrial robot. The Powerhouse also hosts a superb series of exhibitions on a wide range of subjects. Their publishing wing produces an excellent catalogue of books, brochures and CDs, and the shop is packed with interesting objects.

Powerhouse Museum

🍴 Get a foccacia, salad, pasta or an excellent coffee from Lush Bucket at 623 Harris Street. Alternatively, take a bag lunch to Tumbalong Park by Darling Harbour. There are shaded seats outside the Chinese Garden.

🕐 If you think you can get through the collection in one hour, put on your running shoes: entry is free after 4pm.

• Map L5
• 500 Harris St, Darling Harbour
• 9217 0111
• www. powerhousemuseum. com
• Open 10am–5pm daily
• Adult/child/family $10/ $5/$25

Top 10 Exhibits

1. Experimentations
2. Cyberworlds
3. Inspired! Design Across Time
4. EcoLogic
5. Hargrave's Box Kites
6. Kings Cinema
7. Space
8. The Steam Revolution
9. Success & Innovation
10. Transport

1 Experimentations

This interactive exhibit explores scientific and technological break-throughs that have altered our understanding of daily phenomena. Come find out how a battery works, why a freezer door sticks, and much more.

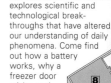

2 Cyberworlds

At this exhibit, meet Robot from the 1960s *Lost in Space* TV series, or chat with Charles Babbage, the inventor of 1832's mechanical computer *(above)*.

3 Inspired! Design Across Time

This new permanent exhibition draws from the museum's extensive collection of Australian and international decorative arts and design, including a Minton & Co. peacock *(left)* from c. 1875.

4 EcoLogic

Sustainable options for houses are explored in this innovative display, which demonstrates the relationship between homes and the natural environment. It examines alternative building approaches and materials, such as recycled timbers and aerated concrete bricks.

Pick up a copy of Ecologic: Creating a Sustainable Future *by Sandra McEwen, available at the Powerhouse Shop.*

5 Hargrave's Box Kites

Lawrence Hargrave *(see p97)* joined four box kites and lifted himself 4.8 m (16 ft) off the ground in 1894. The kites' stability provided the basis for future aircraft designs.

6 Kings Cinema

At this beautiful, miniature Art Deco cinema *(right)*, you might discover old newsreels or enjoy a classic silent film.

7 Space

Find out what it is like to live in space, thanks to a refurbishment of the museum's popular space exhibition. Hear commentary by astronaut Dr. Andy Thomas, and experience the new Zero Gravity Space Lab.

8 The Steam Revolution

Check out the enormous 1785 Boulton and Watt engine *(left)*, the oldest surviving wheel-turning engine in existence. The steam engine actually produces less power than the engine of a small car.

9 Success & Innovation

The computer sock, aluminum pop-top can and black box flight recorder are just some of the Australian inventions profiled here. Don't miss the TV commercial for computer socks featuring "Sir Isaac Newton".

Key

	Level 2
	Level 3
	Level 4
	Level 5

10 Transport

Beneath the Catalina flying boat a collection of railway exhibits includes an old signal box, Locomotive 1243 *(left)* and the destination board used at Central Station from 1906–82.

The Sustainable House

Michael and Heather Mobbs created the "Sustainable House" in 1996, when deciding to renovate their inner-city terrace with minimum environmental impact. It had to generate electricity through solar power, supply water from rainwater tanks and treat its own sewage. In the process, the Mobbs explored everything from the least toxic floor sealants to raising the efficiency of their refrigerator. "EcoLogic" features an interactive 3D model that shows how energy and water are used in the Sustainable House.

Taronga Zoo

The zoo occupies a spectacular setting amidst 28 ha (75 acres) of landscaped bushland overlooking the harbour. Just above the wharf is the Sky Safari, which carries visitors up the hill, over the enclosures and terraced slopes to the lovely Edwardian Entrance Pavilion and Information Centre. The centre provides tour information and brochures describing the zoo's 380 resident species and 2,200 individual animals. Many enclosures recreate natural habitats, such as the Australian Walkabout, which enables visitors to actually experience the animals' original environments. Finally, magical views complement the enjoyable ferry ride returning to Circular Quay.

The Entrance Pavilion

🍴 The Taronga Food Market seats 600 and offers a variety of fare. The zoo's many picnic areas have fantastic views over Sydney Harbour.

✪ Arrive early as many animals are more active in the morning.

- Map F1
- Bradley's Head Rd, Mosman; 9969 2777; Open 9am–5pm daily
- ZooPass adult/child $44/$21–50 (includes return ferry ticket from Circular Quay, admission & Sky Safari ride)
- Tours: 9969 2777; VIP Aussie Gold Tour: 1.5 hrs; adult/child $75/$40; Wild Australian Experience: adult/child $110/$70
- Free Flight Bird Show: 11am & 3pm; Chimpanzee Talk: 1pm; Giraffe Talk: 1:30 pm; Gorilla Feeding: 11am & 2pm; Kids' Zoo: 11.30am; Koala Talk: 3.30pm; Koala Encounters 11am & 2.45pm; Penguin Talk: 2pm; Reptile Talk: 11.30am

Top 10 Exhibits

1. Wild Australia
2. Great Southern Ocean
3. Backyard to Bush
4. African Species
5. Wild Asia
6. Big Cats
7. Primates
8. Serpentaria
9. South American Species
10. Free Flight Bird Show

1 Wild Australia
Meet emus, koalas *(above)*, kangaroos and wallabies in the Australian Walkabout section. The Nocturnal House is home to bilbies, wombats, quolls, platypus and feathertail gliders. Don't miss Ken and his harem in the Koala Walkabout exhibit.

2 Great Southern Ocean
Opened in March 2008, this 3-acre (1.2 ha) precinct houses Taronga's seals, sealions, pelicans and penguins. The exhibit recreates the animals' natural habitat with the glass-fronted enclosure revealing their movements.

3 Backyard to Bush
This innovative exhibit melds the suburban home and the natural environment. Children can engage with farmyard animals at a small farm, and a wombat *(left)* burrow enables a glimpse into the domestic life of these little mammals.

Take the Sky Safari up, get a map, and enjoy a leisurely walk down the terraces and back to the ferry wharf.

African Species
Perched high above Sydney Harbour, the giraffes are one of the many African species at Taronga. The zoo is also home to meerkats, hippopotami, zebras and barbary sheep.

Primates
You don't need the map to find the Gorilla Forest, the Orangutan Rainforest *(below)*, or the Chimpanzee Park: just follow the delighted screams of the youngsters. The rainforest celebrated two chimp births in 2008, one to the big silverback, Kibabu. Check out the primates' outlandish hairstyles as well as their gymnastics.

South American Species
It's hard to ignore the world's largest bird of prey, the Andean condor, the flamboyant Victoria-crowned pigeon, or the antics of the Central American squirrel monkey. The colourful macaws and sun conures are like feathered rainbows.

Free Flight Bird Show
This show features a variety of free flighted birds including Frodo, the barking owl, who joins the Andean Condor, Leslie, and a host of native and exotic species who fly and swoop above the heads of spectators.

Wild Asia
Housing the Zoo's much-loved live Asian elephants, Wild Asia is an experience not to be missed. Follow the leafy trail to see spotted deer, langurs and binturongs. Don't miss seeing the Malaysian tapir swim with otters and coi carp.

Big Cats
Taronga Zoo's big cats – the lions, tigers, snow leopards and fishing cats – are a sight to behold, especially when they enjoy their meals. Take a tour to find out more about these amazing creatures.

Serpentaria
Some of the exhibits here are stunning: the Komodo dragon, the red-eyed tree frog and the Fijian banded iguana for starters. If you enjoy a shiver running down your spine, don't miss Australia's deadly taipan or the South American boa constrictor.

Australian Shark Attack File

The zoo maintains the Australian Shark Attack File. The first recorded fatality was in 1791 on the north coast of NSW. The last fatal attack in Sydney Harbour was in 1963. Don't let this put you off the beaches; they are extremely safe from sharks. Curiously, one of Sydney's most famous crimes, the "shark arm murder", was initially blamed on a shark. A shark captured in 1935 regurgitated a tattooed human arm. The victim was soon identified as a criminal underworld type, James Smith, whose arm had apparently been severed by a knife, not a shark. To this day, no one knows whodunit.

🔟 Bondi Beach

Bondi may just be the most famous stretch of sand in the world. This glorious 1-km (0.6-mile) long sweep of golden sand, with rugged Ben Buckler at its northern end and the Bondi Icebergs to the south, is Sydney's favourite

Statue of a lifesaver

playground, packed with swimmers, surfers and people-watchers alike. Just before the beach is the lively tourist strip Campbell Parade, beyond which is a diverse suburb that embraces surf culture, artists, actors, media tycoons and the vibrant Jewish, Kiwi and Pacific Islander communities. There is some serious money in Bondi, but it's never snobbish and always great fun.

Sign indicating undertow

🍴 For cheap eats with a million-dollar view, get a table on the balcony of the North Bondi Returned Servicemens' League (RSL) at the northern end of the beach.

🛍 Visit Bikini Island at 38 Campbell Parade for a great range of women's swimwear.

- Map H5
- Let's Go Surfing: www.letsgosurfing.com.au
- Beached at Bondi: below the promenade: 9389 5836; towels $4, deck chairs $5, shelters $9, surfboards $15, www.beachedatbondi.com
- Bondi Pavilion Community Cultural Centre: 8362 3400; Open 9:30am–5:30pm Mon–Fri, 10am–5pm Sat-Sun, www.waverley.nsw.gov.au
- Bondi Markets: Bondi Beach Public School; Campbells Parade; Open 10am–5pm Sun, www.bondimarkets.com.au

Top 10 Attractions

1. The Beach
2. Swimming
3. Surfing
4. Ben Buckler
5. Campbell Parade
6. Pavilion
7. Bondi Icebergs
8. Coastal Walk
9. Sculpture by the Sea
10. Surf Lifesavers

The Beach
It's hard to resist this gorgeous arc of golden sand *(right)*, even given how crowded it gets in peak season. Hire a deck chair if towels aren't your thing, and sit back and enjoy the scenery. One of Bondi's great attractions is its varied tribe of devotees.

Swimming
The sand shelves off gently at the northern end of the beach *(above)*, ideal for body surfing. Always swim between the flags. If the weather is on the wild side, leave the water to the surfers and enjoy the Coastal Walk instead.

Surfing
It would be a shame to visit this famous surfing beach without at least trying to catch a wave. The southern end of Bondi Beach is restricted to surfers; boards and wet suits are available for hire nearby. Get a lesson from Let's Go Surfing.

Ben Buckler
If you ever doubted the power of the ocean, check out the rock just below Bondi's northern headland, Ben Buckler. According to its brass plaque, this 240-tonne monster washed up during a storm in 1912. The nearby rock pool is great for children.

Let's go Surfing (see p54) offers surfing lessons for beginners.

5 Campbell Parade
Bondi's main tourist drag *(above)* is always buzzing. Backpackers and tourists rub shoulders with supermodels, surfies and actors. It's a great place for gelati, fish and chips, or a beer overlooking the water.

8 Coastal Walk
Start this spectacular 5-km (3-mile) walk behind the Bondi Icebergs. Follow the path around to Tamarama Beach, also known as "Glamarama" for its "beautiful people". Further down the path is Bronte Beach *(right)*, followed by tiny Clovelly Beach *(see pp48–9)*, Gordon's Bay and Coogee, a less crowded version of Bondi.

10 Surf Lifesavers
Those tanned and athletic men and women patrolling the beach in red and yellow caps *(below)* are members of either Bondi Beach's Surf Bathers' Life Saving Club or North Bondi SLSC. These are two of the oldest clubs in Australia.

6 Pavilion
This 1920s pavilion is home to a lively community cultural centre that hosts movies, theatre, workshops, free art exhibitions and special events. There are also showers and changing rooms inside.

7 Bondi Icebergs
So named because its members swim year round, this clubhouse *(right)* is a Bondi institution. It's home to one of Sydney's finest restaurants *(see p58)* and the world's only surf-life saving museum. Don't miss its saltwater pool washed clean by ocean swells.

9 Sculpture by the Sea
Combine your coastal walk with this annual festival, at which more than 100 artists take full advantage of Bondi's wind-sculpted sandstone headlands as the setting for their works. They are exhibited from late October to November.

Black Sunday
On 6 February 1938, three large waves rolled into Bondi Beach in quick succession. As they receded, hundreds of swimmers were swept out to sea in the backwash. By good fortune, almost 80 members of the Bondi Surf Bathers' Life Saving Club were gathered on the beach in readiness for a competition. Suddenly they were faced with the real thing. Between them, they rescued more than 250 swimmers, which was a remarkable achievement. Unfortunately and despite their best efforts, five swimmers drowned. To this day the tragedy is remembered as Black Sunday.

Left **First Fleet arrives** Centre **The arrest of Governor Bligh** Right **Governor Macquarie**

🔟 Moments in History

1 Aborigines Reach Cadi
The original settlers of Sydney Harbour, the Aboriginal Eora people, arrived almost 50,000 years ago. They fished in the summer months, and during winter they sought food inland and north towards the Hawkesbury River. At the time of white settlement, 1,500 Eora were estimated to live around the Sydney Harbour area.

2 Captain Cook Lands
After observing the Transit of Venus in Tahiti for the Royal Society, Captain James Cook was instructed by the British Admiralty in 1769 to discover and claim the "Great South Continent". He arrived at Botany Bay on 28 April 1770.

3 First Fleet Arrives
Governor Phillip and the First Fleet of 11 ships, carrying 1,500 convicts, guards, military officials and their families, arrived at Botany Bay in 1788. Unable to find sufficient fresh water, Phillip sailed north and found one of the world's "finest harbours". The colony was established at a small cove named in honour of Phillip's neighbour, Viscount Sydney.

4 Rum Corps
The irascible and disliked Governor Bligh threatened to curtail the privileges enjoyed by officers of the NSW "Rum Corps", so named for their use of liquor as a form of currency. They "arrested" Bligh as retaliation in 1808, but their coup was short-lived as they were soon ordered back home to England.

5 Macquarie Takes Charge
Governor Lachlan Macquarie took charge of the colony in 1810 and restored order. During his 12-year governance, he managed to transform the outpost from a ramshackle penal colony into a town with regular roads and civic amenities. He also encouraged Emancipists, convicts who had served their time, to stay and contribute to the colony's growth, thus ensuring a thriving future for Sydney.

6 Dunbar Sinks
On a wild night in 1857, the migrant ship *Dunbar*, en route to Sydney from England, struck rocks near the Heads. Only one passenger survived, while 121 others drowned. It remains Australia's worst ever maritime disaster and came as a bitter blow to the young colony.

7 Troops Set Sail
The first of Australia's World War I volunteers set sail from Sydney Harbour on 1 November 1914, destined for battlefields in Europe and the Middle

Captain James Cook

Mural depicting Green Bans

East. Almost 330,000 Australian troops served overseas and 60,000 died, which was the highest death rate per head of population of all nations involved in the war.

8 Builders' Labourers Impose Green Bans

Several areas, including The Rocks and Woolloomooloo, were saved from developers' wrecking balls in the 1970s. Fortunately for Sydney's future, the Builders' Labourers Federation imposed "Green Bans" on projects that clearly threatened environmentally or historically significant buildings and precincts.

9 Mardi Gras is Born

Over 1,000 gay rights activists took to Sydney's streets demanding equal rights in 1978. Several protestors were arrested, but they vowed to return the following year. The parade that followed in 1979 established an annual event that is now a major tourist attraction (see p72).

10 Cathy Freeman Lights the Olympic Flame

With increasingly more citizens calling for reconciliation between black and white Australia, many rose to their feet when champion Aboriginal runner Cathy Freeman lit the Olympic flame to signal the start of the first Olympic Games of the new millennium in September 2000.

Top 10 Sydney Personalities

1 Pemulwy
This Eora warrior resisted white settlement until he was caught and beheaded in 1802.

2 John & Elizabeth Macarthur
The resourceful Macarthurs established Australia's agricultural industry in 1790.

3 William "Billy" Blue
He started a ferry service between Dawes Point and the North Shore (see p115).

4 Wentworth, Blaxland & Lawson
Opening up Australia's interior, these European explorers crossed the Blue Mountains (see p121) in 1813.

5 Caroline Chisholm
She arrived from Madras in 1838 to establish much-needed services for poor immigrant women.

6 Sir Henry Parkes
A five-time premier of NSW, Parkes was a major proponent of Federation in the late 1800s (see p39).

7 Tilley Devine & Kate Leigh
These madams of crime vied for control of Sydney's 1920s and 30s "razor gangs".

8 Lars Halvorson
This boatbuilder arrived from Norway in 1921 to establish Sydney's most famous boatbuilding dynasty.

9 Jack Mundey
Secretary of the Builders' Labourers Federation, Mundey led the Green Bans (see p85) movement in the 1970s.

10 Ita Buttrose
Indomitable media doyen and former editor-in-chief of the Australian Womens Weekly during the 1970s and 1980s.

Left **Collins Beach** Centre **Mural at Federation Pavilion** Right **Old Government House façade**

Historic Sites & Buildings

1 Aboriginal Rock Art

Several locations around Sydney contain Aboriginal rock art, including Ku-ring-gai Chase National Park *(see p122)*, the Royal National Park *(see p123)*, and the Brisbane Water National Park *(see p127)*. One of the most accessible sites is the North Bondi Golf Course, where you'll find rock carvings just below the tower on Military Road.

2 Captain Cook's Landing Place

Captain James Cook and the crew of the *Endeavour* came ashore at what is now Botany Bay on 29 April 1770. On 6 May they sailed north, soon passing the entrance to a harbour which appeared to offer safe anchorage. Cook named this Port Jackson; it

Captain Cook's landing place

subsequently came to be known as Sydney Harbour. ❧ *Map U5 • Discovery Centre: Captain Cook Drive, Kurnell • 9668 9111 • Open 11am–3pm Mon–Fri, 10am–4:30pm Sat–Sun • Botany Bay National Park: open 7am–7:30pm daily*

3 Tank Stream

The freshwater Tank Stream determined the site of white settlement in 1788. Other than two artworks near Circular Quay *(see p18)*, its only visible remains are in a small display including several items found during excavations, located beneath the old GPO. ❧ *Map M3 • 1 Martin Place • Viewing Room: • lower level • Open 8:15am–5:30pm Mon–Fri, 9am–1pm Sat*

4 Collins Beach

Landing at Collins Beach *(see p118)* in 1790, Governor Phillip and his officers met a group of Aborigines including Bennelong *(see p9)*. An Eora man, never having seen white men before, speared Phillip through the shoulder. Assuming the man had misunderstood his intentions, Philip made no reprisal – that time. ❧ *Map U3*

5 Fort Denison

This small island was once named "Pinchgut" due to the meagre rations doled out to its recidivist convicts. The body of a criminal, Francis Morgan, who was executed in 1796, was left to rot out on the gallows for three years as a warning to new convicts who sailed past the island upon their arrival. ◈ *Map M2* • *NPWS Information Line: 1300 361 967* • *Sydney Harbour Tours: Cadmans Cottage, 110 George St, The Rocks* • *9247 5033* • *Open 9:30am–4:30pm Mon–Fri, 10am–4:30pm Sat–Sun*

Old Government House
Governor Phillip's cottage and country retreat *(see p125)*, constructed in 1790, was rebuilt by Governor Hunter in 1799. Governor and Mrs Macquarie later made numerous alterations to the structure and interior design. The oldest public building in Australia, it is now a National Trust museum. ◈ *Map S3* • *Parramatta Park, Parramatta* • *9635 8149* • *Open 10am–4pm Tue–Fri, 10:30am–4pm Sat & Sun* • *Adm* • *www. nsw.nationaltrust.org.au*

"Granny" Smith Memorial Park
A small park in Eastwood on Sydney's North Shore commemorates Maria "Granny" Smith who, in 1868, discovered in her orchard a mutated variety of apples sprung from the cuttings of French crab apples. Then a curiosity, it soon became the world's best-known variety, particularly valued for its virtues as a cooking apple. ◈ *Map S3* • *Threlfall Street, Eastwood*

Federation Pavilion
Prior to Federation on 1 January 1901, Australia was not a united nation but actually six unaligned and competing colonies, comprising New South Wales, Victoria, Tasmania, Queensland, South Australia and West Australia. This 1988 pavilion in Centennial Park *(see p50)* marks the site of the historic original pavilion, which was right at the centre of celebrations in 1901. ◈ *Map F5*

Manly Beach
Newspaper editor William Gocher challenged the laws in 1902 by enjoying a midday swim at Manly *(see p118)*. His crime? It was illegal to swim in public between 6am and 8pm. Thanks to Gocher's bold action, daylight bathing was legalised within a year, provided that one always wore a conservative neck-to-knee swimsuit. ◈ *Map U3*

Sydney Olympic Park
Many events of the 2000 Olympic Games, including the opening and closing ceremonies, took place at Sydney Olympic Park *(see pp52–53)*, 14 km (8.5 miles) west of the city. The park also contains the Tennis Centre, the Aquatic Centre and the Sydney Showgrounds. The Visitor Gateway provides maps and runs tours. ◈ *Map S4* • *Homebush Bay* • *www.sydneyolympicpark.com.au* • *Visitor Gateway (next to Olympic Park railway station): 1 Showground Rd* • *9714 7888* • *Open 9am–5pm daily*

Left **May Gibbs' studio at Nutcote** Right **Henry Lawson**

Writers

1 Patrick White (1912–90)

Australia's Nobel prize-winning author for the *Eye of the Storm* (1973) hailed from a family of wealthy Australian pastoralists. He spent much of his early life in Europe but settled near Centennial Park *(see p50)* in 1964. Although he wrote poetry and plays, he is best remembered for his novels, which often explore individuals' efforts to divine meaning from the circumstances of their lives.

2 Kylie Tennant (1912–88)

Best known for her 1943 novel *Ride on Stranger*, Kylie Tennant often presented life from the perspective of the disposessed. Despite her later success as an author, reviewer and lecturer, Tennant also experienced life on the other side of the tracks, including a short stint in jail in the 1930s.

Kylie Tennant

3 Frank Moorhouse (b. 1938)

His early stories focused on middle-class, small-town Australia, demonstrating his affinity with the "new journalism" of Americans such as Tom Wolfe. *Grand Days* and *Dark Palace* trace the aspirations and disappointments of the League of Nations through the eyes of an Australian woman.

4 Peter Corris (b. 1942)

Sydney's Raymond Chandler, Peter Corris writes hard-boiled crime fiction set in and around Sydney. His main protagonist, Cliff Hardy, is a private detective forever sorting through the trash of the powerful and wealthy.

5 Kenneth Slessor (1901–71)

Poet Kenneth Slessor will always be remembered for his 1939 elegy "Five Bells", written for a friend who drowned. Another poem, "Beach Burial" (1944), written while serving as a war correspondent near El Alamein, describes the burial of sailors washed up on shore after battles in the Mediterranean.

6 May Gibbs (1876–1969)

May Gibbs wrote and illustrated children's stories that were distinguished for their inventiveness and their use of Australian flora and fauna. Nutcote *(see p116)*, her home for more than 40 years, is now a museum dedicated to her work.

7 Miles Franklin (1879–1954)
Franklin struggled for years following the success of her 1901 novel, *My Brilliant Career*, but found renewed interest in 1928 when she published *Up the Country*. She was an early feminist and worked with women's groups in the USA and as a nurse in Europe during World War I. Upon her death, her estate established Australia's most prestigious literary award, named in her honour.

8 Henry Lawson (1867–1922)
Lawson's writing is often humorous and inspired by romantic notions of the Australian "character". In stories such as 1892's *The Drover's Wife* he exalted the "mateship" of rural Australians surviving the harsh and isolated environment. He often led an itinerant life and struggled with alcoholism. He was the first Australian writer granted a state funeral.

9 Ruth Park (b 1923)
Park's two most famous novels, *The Harp in the South*, (1948) and its sequel *Poor Man's Orange* (1949), explored life in 1930s Surry Hills, which was then one of Sydney's poorest slums. She is also a prolific children's author and penned the much-loved Muddle-Headed Wombat series.

10 Thomas Keneally (b 1935)
Keneally is a prolific and prize-winning author who has had several of his historical novels translated into film. His subjects have ranged from Aboriginal resistance in *The Chant of Jimmy Blacksmith* (1972), to the Holocaust, in 1982's *Schindler's Ark*.

Top 10 Novels set in Sydney

1 A Timeless Land (1941)
This novel by Eleanor Dark includes several historical Sydney characters.

2 Come in Spinner (1951)
By Dymphna Cusack and Florence James. A group of Sydney women are thrown into turmoil during WWII.

3 They're a Weird Mob (1957)
Memoirs of John O'Grady, an "Italian immigrant journalist" turned builders' labourer.

4 Riders in the Chariot (1961)
A satire by Patrick White.

5 Careful He Might Hear You (1963)
By Sumner Locke Elliot. A 1930s orphan resists his aunt's efforts to adopt him.

6 The Glass Canoe (1976)
David Ireland's darkly comic novel is set in the masculine world of a suburban pub.

7 Puberty Blues (1979)
A coming-of-age 1970s beach culture story by Kathy Lette and Gabrielle Carey.

8 Oscar and Lucinda (1988)
This Booker Prize-winning novel by Peter Carey traces a romance between a gambling minister and an heiress.

9 Looking for Alibrandi (1992)
Melina Marchetta's coming-of-age novel features a young girl struggling to find her identity.

10 Monkey's Mask (1994)
Dorothy Porter's verse novel features a lesbian private detective and several poetic red herrings.

Left **Exhibit at the Australian Museum** Centre **Maritime Museum** Right **Susannah Place shop**

🔟 Museums

1 Museum of Sydney

The MOS *(see p77)* is located on the site of the first interaction between Sydney's Cadigal people and the British First Fleet. See what the city looked like 100 years ago and discover the history of its indigenous people. ⬙ *Map N2 • Phillip & Bridge Sts • 9251 5988 • Open 9:30am–5pm daily • Dis access • Adm*

2 Australian Museum

Established in 1827, Australia's first museum is the place to explore the country's natural and cultural history through its huge collection of artifacts. Experience indigenous culture with dance performance every Sunday, and enjoy interactive features for kids and inspired temporary exhibitions. ⬙ *Map N4 • 6 College St • 9320 6000 • Open 9:30am–5pm daily • Dis access • Adm*

Endeavour, Maritime Museum

3 Powerhouse Museum

This museum of science, design and technology is interesting and great fun, offering many interactive displays *(see pp30–31)*.

Powerhouse Museum

4 Hyde Park Barracks Museum

In Francis Greenway's historic building, this museum *(see p22)* uses objects, soundscapes and testimonies to recreate the lives of convicts in early Sydney. Learn about their crimes, their difficult voyage from England and their rebuilding of the colony. Then have a look at the dormitory hammocks. ⬙ *Map N3 • Queens Sq, Macquarie St • 8239 2311 • Open 9:30am–5pm daily • Adm*

5 National Maritime Museum

Darling Harbour is the ideal spot for this museum *(see p28)* dedicated to life at sea. From the watercraft of indigenous Australians to the history of the Royal Australian Navy, the museum has it all covered. It is possible to tour some of the historic boats moored nearby including the replica of Cook's *Endeavour*. ⬙ *Map L3 • 2 Murray St, Darling Harbour • 9298 3777 • Open 9:30am–5pm daily • Dis access*

6 Sydney Jewish Museum

This museum traces the history of Jewish life in Sydney, from a tiny group who arrived on the First Fleet in the 18th century to today's thriving community of over 30,000. There is also a Holocaust memorial and section, tours of which can be arranged *(see p85)*.

The Historic Houses Trust manages many museums. If you plan to visit lots of them, a Ticket Through Time offers great value.

Montage at the Justice & Police Museum

Justice & Police Museum
Sydney's convict past was the start of a colourful history of crime and prosecution. Find out about the thugs of the past, the heroic cops who caught them and Sydney's current underworld. The museum has a vast collection of police and judicial evidence such as court records and mug shots. ◈ Map N2 • Phillip & Albert Sts, Circular Quay • 9252 1144 • Open 10am–5pm Sat–Sun (daily during NSW school holidays)

Susannah Place Museum
Built in 1844, Susannah Place Museum is as much a historic site as it is a museum; the row of quaint terrace houses evokes life in early Sydney. The houses have the city's oldest original outdoor laundries and brick lavatories. One of the houses has been recreated as a corner shop that sells goods from that historical era. ◈ Map M2 • 58–64 Gloucester St, The Rocks • 9241 1893 • Open 10am–5pm Sat–Sun (daily during NSW school holidays) • By guided tour only, every half hour • Adm

Nicholson Museum
In Sydney University's (see p103) Gothic sandstone Quadrangle, the Nicholson Museum building is worth visiting for its architecture alone. It's a fitting venue for an impressive collection of antiquities, including a large range of Eastern Mediterranean artifacts. ◈ Map C5 • Southern Entrance, Main Quadrangle, University of Sydney • 9351 2812 • Open 10am–4:30pm Mon–Fri, noon–4pm Sun • www.usyd.edu.au/museums

Macleay Museum
Also at the University of Sydney (see p103), Macleay Museum was built in 1887 to house the vast entomological collection of the Macleay family. Since then, the collection has been added to by various ethnographers, naturalists and anthropologists. The pieces exhibited were mostly collected in the 1870s and include the oldest Aboriginal bark paintings in existence. The collection now includes over 1,000 antique scientific instruments. ◈ Map C5 • Gosper Lane, University of Sydney • 9036 5853 • Open 10am–4.30pm Mon–Fri, noon–4pm Sun • www.usyd.edu.au/museums

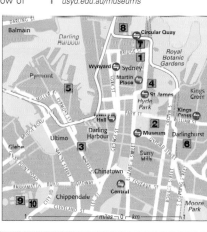

A Ticket Through Time allows unlimited entry for three months to 13 HHT properties and museums.

43

Left **AGNSW** Centre **Brett Whiteley Studio** Right **Australian Centre for Photography**

Art Galleries

1 Art Gallery of NSW
It's easy to spend a whole day in Sydney's most extensive art gallery *(see pp24–7)*.

2 Museum of Contemporary Art
This 1950s mock Art Deco edifice housed the Maritime Services Board until it became a gallery in 1991. The MCA displays the best of international art. ⦿ *Map M2 • Circular Quay West • 9245 2400 • Open 10am–5pm daily • Closed 25 Dec • www.mca.com.au • Dis access*

3 Object
Also known as the Australian Centre for Craft and Design, this gallery exhibits works by textile designers, jewellers, furniture designers, ceramicists and glass-blowers, demonstrating crafts as real art forms. Its store sells a great range of limited edition design-pieces. ⦿ *Map N6 • Gallery 417: Bourke St, Surry Hills • 9361 4511 • Open 11am–6pm Tue–Sun • www. object.com.au • Dis access*

4 Artspace
A non-commercial gallery, Artspace presents contemporary works. Some shows include traditional artforms such as painting, but many lean towards the experimental through new media, installations and performance. ⦿ *Map P3 • 43–51 Cowper Wharf Rd, Woolloomooloo • 9356 0555 • Open 11am–5pm Tue–Sat, 11am–8pm Thu • www.artspace.org.au • Dis access*

5 Brett Whiteley Studio
When Brett Whiteley died in 1992, his wife turned his studio into a memorial *(see pp26 & 93)*. Now an adjunct of the AGNSW, his bedroom and workspace have been left intact. Get to know the artist through his unfinished paintings or the gallery space that exhibits his work. ⦿ *Map N6 • 2 Raper St, Surry Hills • 9225 1881 • Open 10am–4pm Sat–Sun • www.brettwhiteley.org • Adm*

6 SH Ervin Gallery
Enjoy a unique Australian art experience at one of Sydney's premier galleries. Set in heritage surrounds, the programme features changing exhibitions, weekly talks and guest speakers. ⦿ *Map M1 • Watson Rd, Observatory Hill, The Rocks • 9258 0173 • Open 11am–5pm Tue–Sun • www.nsw.nationaltrust.org.au • Adm*

Interior wall of the Brett Whiteley Studio

The MCA offers free guided tours at 11am Mon–Fri, noon Sat–Sun

7 Australian Centre for Photography

Founded in 1973, Australia's longest established contemporary gallery presents the best in local and international photography and new media. A photo wall features works by emerging artists, while the main space contains temporary exhibitions. ✆ *Map Q6 • 257 Oxford St, Paddington • 9332 1455 • Open noon–7pm Tue–Fri, 10am–6pm Sat & Sun • www.acp.au.com*

8 Gavala Aboriginal Art Centre

This is Sydney's only Aboriginal art gallery owned by Indigenous people. Combining an exhibition space with a shop, Gavala offers storytelling, didgeridoo-playing demonstrations and Aboriginal artists-in-residence who discuss their work. ✆ *Map L4 • Ground Floor, Shop 131, Harbourside Shopping Centre, Darling Harbour • 9212 7232 • Open 10am–9pm daily • Dis access • www.gavala.com.au*

9 2 Danks Street

Home to ten commercial galleries displaying a wide range of art, this converted warehouse is a forerunner of the new arty precinct southeast of the CBD. German Conny Dietzschold shows exciting international art, Utopia exhibits Aboriginal art and Gow Langsford presents a range of international art. ✆ *Map D5 • 2 Danks St, Waterloo • 9318 0404 • Open 11am–6pm Tue–Sat • Dis access • www.2danksstreet.com.au*

10 State Library Galleries

Exhibitions are presented in five galleries. The Library hosts photography, collection treasures, and historical material *(see p22)*. ✆ *Map N3 • 9273 1414 • Open 9am–8pm Mon–Thu, 9am–5pm Fri, 10am–5pm Sat & Sun • Dis access • www.sl.nsw.gov.au*

Top 10 Paddington Private Galleries

1 Sherman Galleries
Exhibits top contemporary Australian artists. ✆ *Map Q6 • 16–20 Goodhope St • 9331 1112*

2 Roslyn Oxley9
Renowned contemporary Australian artists. ✆ *Map R6 • 8 Soudan Lane • 9331 1919*

3 Tim Olsen Gallery
Works by John Olsen and other contemporary Australian artists. ✆ *Map F5 • 63 Jersey Rd • 9327 3922*

4 Australian Galleries
Contemporary Australian works by artists such as Jeffery Smart. ✆ *Map R6 • 15 Roylston St • 9360 5177 • Works On Paper: 24 Glenmore Rd • 9380 8744*

5 Hogarth Galleries
Deals in Aboriginal art, sourcing work from Australia's far north. ✆ *Map Q6 • 7 Walker Lane • 9000 0000*

6 Blender Gallery
Specialises in photography. ✆ *Map R6 • 16 Elizabeth St • 9380 7080*

7 Stills Gallery
A wide range of Australian photography. ✆ *Map Q5 • 36 Gosbell St • 9331 7775*

8 Kaliman Gallery
Contemporary Australian art. ✆ *Map R6 • 56 Sutherland St, Paddington • 9357 2273*

9 Eva Breuer Art Dealer
A conservative collection of Australian art from every period. ✆ *Map F5 • 83 Moncur St, Woollahra • 9362 0297*

10 Maunsell Wickes
Mid career and young emerging artists cover a range of art practices. ✆ *Map E4 • 19 Glenmore Rd, Paddington • 9331 4676 • www.maunsellwickes.com*

The monthly magazine *Art in Australia* lists countrywide exhibitions and is available at most galleries.

Left **Sydney Opera House against the city skyline** Right **Walsh Bay**

TOP 10 Architectural Highlights

1 Sydney Opera House

If you only manage to explore one building in Sydney, make it this one. Not simply beautiful from afar, a close look at the shells' interior reveals the complexity of the gravity-defying construction. Renovations are underway to realise Jørn Utzon's original vision for the interiors. See pp8–11

2 Sydney Theatre & Walsh Bay

The Walsh Bay wharves recently became the first World Heritage-listed urban site in Australia. They have been reinvigorated as an elegant new precinct made up of theatres, restaurants, a hotel and apartments. Shipping timbers and dock machinery have been incorporated into the new buildings. Map M1
• Pier 4, 22 Hickson Rd, Walsh Bay

3 Aurora Place

The ethereal white glass skin and sails atop Renzo Piano's office block and apartment buildings, built in 2000, echo the Opera House's shells and the spinnakers of yachts on the harbour. They also regulate the temperature, making the skyscraper one of the most energy-efficient buildings in the CBD. Map N3
• 88 Phillip St

4 Governor Phillip Tower

Part of a large development on a historic site, the base of this elegant high-rise carefully slopes over several 19th-century terrace houses. The neighbouring Museum of Sydney (see p42) preserves the footings of the first Government House. In *Mission Impossible 2*, Tom Cruise abseiled through the roof's steel blades. Map M3 • 1 Farrer Place

5 Altair

Designed by Sydney's arbiters of style, Engelen Moore, Altair was voted the world's best apartment building in 2001. The coup was clinched by its environmental performance and sleek lines. Mechanical louvres on the building's façade open to catch the breeze. Map Q5
• 3 Kings Cross Rd, Rushcutters Bay

6 Australia Square

Built in the 1960s, this structure was a revisioning of Sydney's downtown, combining office, retail and public space. Today the building is still revered as a marvel of concrete construction. Architect Harry Seidler chamfered the building's corners to reduce its shadow, giving the tower its iconic round form. Map M3 • 264–278 George St • Adm

Governor Phillip Tower

Sydney Architecture Walks runs excellent tours of architecture and public art. Visit www.sydneyarchitecture.org

7 Republic 2

Over-scaled openings animate the grand façade of this cool white apartment complex, designed by the architectural style gurus Burley Katon Halliday. The large apartments are situated around a sunny, stone-paved courtyard, complete with sculpture and a great breakfast café. ❧ Map P5 • 46–50 Burton St, Darlinghurst

8 Rose Seidler House

Sydney's most significant architect, whose work spans over 50 years, Harry Seidler was almost single-handedly responsible for bringing Bauhaus and European Modernism to Australia. This modest but lovely house, commissioned by Seidler's mother in 1950, assimilates the best Modernist features. Also check out its interesting collection of original furniture and appliances. ❧ Map T2 • 71 Clissold Rd, Wahroonga • Open 10am–5pm Sun • 9989 8020

9 Aussie Stadium

The roof of this stadium (see p53) is a low-slung "Mexican hat" which allows tantalising glimpses of sports crowds from nearby Fox Studios. Designed by local architect Phillip Cox, it was built to coincide with Sydney's Bicentenary in 1988. ❧ Map E5 • Driver Ave, Moore Park

10 Homebush Train Station

Not often is a station so architecturally interesting: this one is a rare beast. Supporting a delicate membrane roof, 18 vaulted arches hover over the rail platform and provide an impressive gateway to the extensive Homebush sporting complex (see pp52–53). ❧ Map S4 • Olympic Park, Homebush

Top 10 Public Art

1 Edge of the Trees
Janet Laurence and Fiona Foley. Symbolises reconciliation with Aborigines (see p77). ❧ Museum of Sydney

2 Almost Once
Brett Whiteley. ❧ AGNSW

3 Federation Pavilion
Alexander Tzannes and Imants Tillers. Built for the Bicentenary celebrations. ❧ Centennial Park

4 Veil of Trees
Janet Laurence and Jisuk Han. Ethereal images on glass reflect the changing light. ❧ The Domain

5 Magnolia & Palm
Bronwyn Oliver. Giant seeds recall botanical studies by Australia's explorers. ❧ Botanic Gardens

6 Dual Nature
Nigel Helyer. Whimsical structures play with the tides. ❧ Woolloomooloo Bay

7 Wuganmagulya
Brenda L Croft. Describes the significance of the Botanic Gardens to the Aborigines. ❧ Botanic Gardens

8 Memory is Creation Without End
Kimio Tsuchiya. Sandstone blocks from demolished buildings are strewn on the grass. ❧ Tarpeian Way, South Domain

9 Tankstream
Lynne Roberts-Goodwin. Marks the the colony's original water supply (see p18). ❧ Pitt Street Mall to Alfred St

10 Tied To Tide
Jennifer Turpin and Michaelie Crawford. A dynamic sculpture that responds to water levels. ❧ Pyrmont Bay Park, Pirrama Rd, Pyrmont

Sydney's Top 10

The Eastern Suburb's crescent-shaped Bondi Beach

Beaches

1 Bondi
Australia's most famous beach is a perfect crescent of sand with good surfing spots at either end, and usually calm enough for a swim in the middle. Being so close to the city, it won't take too long to get your toes wet *(see pp34–35)*.

2 Manly
On the peninsula's ocean side, this popular long beach *(see p118)* is the homeground of many of Australia's ironmen and women, and the site of surf lifesaving championships. The esplanade is good for jogging and rollerblading, and goes all the way round to lovely, sheltered Shelly Beach.

3 Palm
An hour and a half's drive north of Sydney, the area around this beach is a magnet for the city's glitterati. "Palmie" is a lovely beach fringed by pine trees, and was made famous by the soap opera *Home and Away*. For a cruisy afternoon, catch the Pittwater ferry for a loop around the bay *(see p122)*.

Pelicans at Palm Beach

4 Cronulla
This beach in the southern suburbs was immortalised in *Puberty Blues*. Still a grommet (young surfer wannabes) training ground, it hasn't lost any of its teen appeal. Grab a chiko roll and get into the spirit. ◈ *Map T6*

5 Maroubra
The Eastern Suburbs' most serious surf beach has big waves and a wide stretch of sand. When you're done with the water, walk round the coast to see a series of rockpools brimming with sealife. Maroubra offers good facilities such as a shaded playground, changing rooms and a kiosk. ◈ *Map U5*

6 Clontarf
This harbour beach is wonderful for small children. There's plenty of shade, a playground, a shallow tidal pool, and a great view of yachts moving to and from the marina opposite. After your swim, satisfy your hunger across the bay at The Spit with a satisfying plate of fish and chips. ◈ *Map U3*

7 Balmoral
Another excellent children's beach, Balmoral has a large enclosure of shark nets bordered by a wooden boardwalk which kids love to jump off. Grassy picnic areas abound, the water is warm and calm, and there are many places to buy the kids an ice cream. ◈ *Map U3*

For Security and Health tips, see p137.

Bronte's swimming baths

8 Bronte
The picnic area at this small beach is dotted with little huts that provide picnic tables and shelter from the wind. On the weekends it's packed with groups of 20-somethings enjoying barbecues and beer. Bronte also boasts a great ocean pool and a fabulous row of cafés. ⊗ *Map G6*

9 Clovelly
If you walk between the cliffs that separate Bronte and Clovelly, you'll pass through Waverley Cemetery, where Aussie poet Henry Lawson *(see p41)* rests. Due to its backwater, Clovelly's waters are very calm, making it wonderful for laps and snorkelling. ⊗ *Map U4*

10 Nielsen Park
On summer weekends, this sheltered harbour beach is packed with picnicking families. The adjacent park *(see p51)* has good spots for cricket or frisbee. Small children can safely play in the water, but keep in mind that the harbour floor dips away suddenly. ⊗ *Map G2*

Top 10 Swimming Pools

1 Andrew "Boy" Charlton
Sydney's style set love the slick renovation *(see p20)*. Outdoor, saltwater. ⊗ *The Domain • 9358 6686*

2 Sydney Olympic Park Aquatic Centre
Facilities include a water park for kids *(see p52)*. Indoor. ⊗ *Olympic Boulevard, Sydney Olympic Park • 9752 3666*

3 Cook & Phillip Park
In the heart of the CBD; also has a gym. Indoor. ⊗ *4 College St • 9326 0444*

4 North Sydney Olympic
Swim looking up at the Harbour Bridge. Indoor and outdoor. ⊗ *4 Alfred St South, Milsons Point • 9955 2309*

5 Bondi Icebergs
The home of winter swimming since 1929 *(see p25)*. Outdoor. ⊗ *1 Notts Ave, Bondi Beach • 9130 4804*

6 Dawn Fraser Pool
See where the world record breaker got her start. Outdoor, saltwater. ⊗ *Fitzroy Ave, Balmain • 9555 1903*

7 Wylie's Baths
Popular ocean rock pool. ⊗ *Neptune St, Coogee*

8 McIver's Baths
Coogee's women-only pool, a favourite of the lesbian community. Ocean rock pool. ⊗ *Neptune St, Coogee*

9 Fairy Bower
Tiny, with incredible views over the Pacific. Ocean rock pool. ⊗ *Bower St, Manly*

10 Forty Baskets Beach
Only accessible down stairs through the bush, and worth it for the peace and views of Manly. Tidal harbour pool. ⊗ *Balgowlah Hts*

Left **Basking in the sun at Centennial Park**

Parks & Gardens

1 Bradleys Head

Walking trails take you around the tip of one of Sydney Harbour National Park's highlights, where you can often spot noisy flocks of rainbow lorikeets. At the end of the headland is the tripod mast of the original HMAS *Sydney (see p13)* and a small Doric column marking one nautical mile from Fort Denison *(see p38)*. ✪ Map F2

2 Centennial Park

Sydney's Central Park is a gorgeous 220-ha (543-acre) expanse of playing fields, horse-riding facilities *(see pp54 & 57)*, ornamental lakes and ponds, cultivated gardens, sports grounds, cycle and jogging paths and light bushland with beautiful paperbark trees. It is the largest open space in the central area and a popular destination for barbecues and picnics. ✪ Map E5

3 Garigal National Park

This rainforest zone on the North Shore may offer you the best chance to spy the elusive lyrebird in its natural habitat. You will also find tree ferns and cabbage tree palms *(Livistonia Australis)*, which were used by white settlers for everything from hats to building materials. ✪ Map T3

Giant chess board at Hyde Park

4 Hyde Park

Standing at the edge of the city centre, this formal park provides a respite from the city's bustle. It features a magnificent avenue of figs, the Art Deco Archibald Fountain at its northern end and the Anzac Memorial *(see p78)*. A site for public executions in 1802, only one year later it was used for Sydney's first cricket match. Australia's first horse race was run here in 1810. ✪ Map N4

5 Lane Cove National Park

The park follows Lane Cove River, which flows into Sydney Harbour. Here you'll find echidnas, sugar gliders, mangroves, dusky moorhens, sheltered gullies and open eucalypt forests with stately Sydney red gums *(Angophora costata)* growing out of the sandstone. At dusk their smooth pink bark is almost luminous. ✪ Map S3

Red gum tree at Lane Cove

Left **Greycliffe House at Nielson Park** Right **North Head's Shelly Beach**

6 Arthur McElhone Reserve

Tucked below Kings Cross, this tiny manicured park is located in Elizabeth Bay (see p86). It has a stone bridge over a trickling pond filled with Koi, and magnificent views of the yachts moored in Rushcutters Bay and the ritzy Eastern Suburbs enclave of Darling Point. ⚲ Map Q3

7 Nielsen Park

Overlooking Shark Bay, this park (see p49) has been a Sydney favourite since 1912. At its north end is Shark Beach and the historic Greycliffe House (see 98). To the west is Steel Point, site of a former defensive battery, and the start of the 1.5-km (1-mile) Hermitage Foreshore Walk back to Rose Bay.

8 North Head

The more rugged of the two Heads, this section of the Sydney Harbour National Park features windswept heathlands, shaded gullies, secluded Collins Beach and the Old Quarantine Station (see p110). Pretty Cabbage Tree Bay and Shelly Beach (see p118) are to the north. ⚲ Map U3

9 Observatory Park

Given its location beside the southern approach to the Sydney Harbour Bridge, this small park below the Observatory (see p19) is surprisingly peaceful. It offers great views of the working harbour. Near the bandstand is a memorial to the Australians who served in the South African War (1899–1902). ⚲ Map D3

10 South Head

Governor Phillip spent his first night in Sydney Harbour, 22 January 1788, inside South Head (see p98). The headland features the red-and-white striped Hornby Lighthouse, so-painted to distinguish it from the Macquarie Lighthouse. It's a prime vantage spot for viewing the Sydney to Hobart yacht race (see p73).

Left **Track events at Sydney Olympic Park** Right **Sydney Cricket Ground**

Sporting Venues & Olympic Sites

1 ANZ Stadium

Sydney's largest stadium was designed as the centerpiece of the 2000 Sydney Olympics. Millions tuned in to watch this venue's opening and closing ceremonies and athletics events. The stadium seats over 80,000 and hosts Australian Rules football, Rugby League and Union, soccer and cricket. ◉ *Map S4 • Sydney Olympic Park • 8765 2000 • www.anzstadium.com.au*

2 Sydney Olympic Park Aquatic Centre

Australia prides itself on its competitive swimmers, and the Aquatic Centre is a testament to this national obsession. The centre includes a water park and the main competition pool, which accommodates short and long course swimming, water polo, synchronized swimming and underwater hockey. A sauna, steam room, river rapid ride, spray jets, bubble beach, five spas, spurting volcanoes and water slides will keep the whole family happy. ◉ *Map S4 • Sydney Olympic Park • 9752 3666 • www.aquaticcentre.com.au*

Sydney Olympic Park Aquatic Centre

3 Sydney Olympic Park Tennis Centre

Built on an old horse stud-farm, this complex was designed in consultation with Australian tennis pro John Newcombe and the creators of Wimbledon's Court 1. It features a centrepiece circular centre court with shade cover, two show courts, seven match courts and six practice courts, all surfaced with Rebound Ace. Special loops aid those with hearing impairments. ◉ *Map S4 • Sydney Olympic Park • 9764 1999 • www.sydneytennis.com.au*

4 Sydney Olympic Park Hockey Centre

The unique grandstand roof of this centre is suspended from a single mast, giving the 4,000 spectators an uninterrupted view of the entire pitch. The world-class venue is home to NSW state hockey, and also plays host to gridiron, touch football, Oz tag and lacrosse. ◉ *Map S4 • Sydney Olympic Park • 9763 0111 • sscbay.nsw.gov.au/minigen*

5 Royal Randwick Racecourse

First established in 1833 as "Sandy Course", it became known as Royal Randwick in 1992. The racecourse is a lush green surface surrounded by charming old stands. Autumn and Spring Racing Carnivals attract large crowds to watch Australia's top horses in action. ◉ *Map E6 • Alison Rd, Randwick • 9663 8400 • www.ajc.org.au*

The SCG Tour Experience runs guided tours of the SCG and Aussie Stadium at 10am & 1pm Mon–Fri & 10am Sat; call 1300 724 737.

6 Showgrounds Exhibition Building

From Royal Easter Shows to international baseball games and rock concerts, this site has hosted them all. The Showground features a main arena, a Clydesdale pavilion inspired by the architecture of 18th- and 19th-century English churches, an open-air woodchop stadium and numerous pavilions. ✆ Map S4
• Sydney Olympic Park • 9704 1111
• www.sydneyshowground.com.au

7 Acer Arena

Seating 21,000 people, the Superdome is the largest indoor entertainment and sporting arena in Australia. One of the major venues for the 2000 Sydney Olympics, the venue hosted the basketball finals, artistic gymnastics, trampoline and wheelchair basketball. ✆ Map S4
• Sydney Olympic Park • 8765 4321
• www.acerarena.com.au

8 Sydney Cricket Ground

This area was granted to the British Army in 1851 (see p92). In 1870 Rugby Union was first played here. Today, the hallowed turf hosts cricket in the summer, Australian Rules Football in the winter, and various sports and concerts in between. ✆ Map E5
• Moore Park Rd, Paddington • 9360 6601
• www.sydneycricketground.com.au

9 Aussie Stadium

Home of the Sydney Roosters RLC, the NSW Waratahs and the Sydney FC, Aussie Stadium, the former Sydney Football Stadium, is adjacent to the Sydney Cricket Ground. ✆ Map E5 • Moore Park Rd, Paddington • 9360 6601 • www.aussiestadium.com.au

10 Sydney Entertainment Centre

Known to fans of the Sydney Kings basketball team as "the Kingdome", this is the large home venue for a team who ride a wave of popular local support. The centre also hosts concerts and shows, often presenting some of the biggest names in entertainment. ✆ Map L5 • 35 Harbour St, Darling Harbour • 9320 4200
• www.sydentcent.com.au

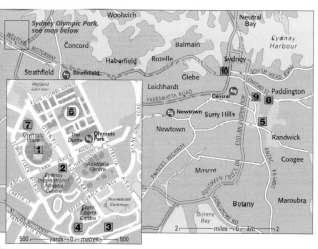

The Novotel's top-floor viewing room gives a breathtaking view of the Olympic site and its surrounds.

Left **Boating at the Royal National Park** Right **Horseriding at Centennial Park**

🔟 Outdoor Activities

1 Swimming & Surfing

Sydney has dozens of beaches and most are safe for swimming. The harbour beaches are generally calm, good for a relaxing paddle and for children. The ocean beaches *(see pp48–9)* are likely to have a rougher swell, perfect for surfing, body-boarding and body-surfing; you can take lessons at Let's Go Surfing. At ocean beaches, make sure to swim between the flags, in the lifeguard-patrolled area. ⬧ *Let's Go Surfing: Map H5 • 128 Ramsgate Ave, North Bondi • 9365 1800 • www.letsgosurfing.com.au*

2 Kayaking

Get up close to Middle Harbour's mansions by kayaking around the foreshore. While the more energetic prefer to join the fast-paced traffic of the harbour, others can slowly drift along simply admiring the view.
⬧ *Sydney Harbour Kayaks: Map U3 • The Spit Bridge, Mosman • 9960 4389 • www.sydneyharbourkayaks.com.au*

3 Cycling

There are dedicated cycle tracks in Centennial Park and in streets throughout Sydney. For a real cycling adventure, take a tour of the foreshore and ride across the Harbour Bridge, or mountain bike down the lovely Blue Mountains *(see p121)* with Boomerang Bicycle Tours. ⬧ *Bike Hire: Woolys Wheels • Map P6 • 82 Oxford St, Paddington • 9331 2671 • Cycle maps: www.rta.nsw.gov.au • Boomerang Bicycle Tours: 9890 1996*

4 Horseriding

Centennial Park has a show-jumping area and a dedicated equestrian track that runs the 3.6 km (2.2 miles) around the park. Escorted park rides and lessons in dressage and jumping are available from Centennial and Moore Park Stables. ⬧ *Centennial Stables: Map E5 • Cook & Lang Rds, Centennial Park • 9360 5650 • Moore Park Stables: Map E5 • 9360 8747*

5 Golf

Many of the city's golf courses are private, but there are also some good public ones. Moore Park's is a championship 18-hole, par-70 course close to the CBD. There is also a three-tiered driving range, floodlit at night. ⬧ *Moore Park: Map E5 • Anzac Parade & Cleveland St • 9663 1064 • Open dawn–10pm • www.mooreparkgolf.com.au*

Cycling at Centennial Park

⬅ *Protect yourself from UV rays and dehydration by applying sunscreen, wearing a hat and sunglasses and carrying water.*

Bushwalking

6 Bushwalking
Sydney may be a bustling city, but the bush is just a short train ride away. There are 24 national parks in and around Sydney (see pp50–51), and all offer excellent bushwalks of varying experience levels. Take a guided tour with the NPWS and learn all about native animals and bush foods. ◉ NPWS: 1300 361 967 • www.nationalparks.nsw.gov.au

7 Waterskiing
The idyllic environs of the Hawkesbury River (see121) make it one of the most popular locations for watersports. Try waterskiing, wakeboarding, kneeboarding or barefooting with a lesson at Sydney Waterski and Wakeboard; they cater to all levels of experience. Pickups from train stations or the CBD can be easily arranged. ◉ Sydney Waterski and Wakeboard: 0418 633 106 • www.sydneywaterski.com.au

8 Ballooning
Dawn balloon flights over the Sydney region are a great experience, tranquil yet exhilarating, with lovely views of the sprawling city and the hazy Blue Mountains. Weather permitting, Balloon Aloft offers daily flights from Camden, followed by a barbecue and champagne breakfast. Ballooning might not be appropriate for those scared of heights. ◉ Balloon Aloft: 1800 028 568 • www.balloonaloft.com

9 Sailing
Charter a skippered yacht and relax as you sail around the harbour, or navigate yourself and up to seven friends in a 6.1-m (20-ft) cruiser. Hiring a 20-footer includes a fishing license and costs $360 for 4 hours or $675 for 8 hours. ◉ Sydney Harbour Escapes: Map G3 • Rose Bay Marina, New South Head Rd, Rose Bay • 9328 4718

10 Barefoot Bowls & Beer
It may be every Aussie grandma's pastime, but it has also been recently undergoing a surge in popularity, thanks mainly to the patronage of certain Sydney celebrities and a bunch of trendy kids. Try the original and the best, Sunday arvo bowls at Paddington Bowling Club. ◉ Paddington Bowling Club: 9363 1150

Sailing on Sydney Harbour

The City to Surf is a 14-km (8.7-mile) run weaving through Sydney, from William Street to Bondi Beach via Heartbreak Hill.

The famous laughing clown face welcomes visitors to Luna Park

Activities for Children

Opening poster for Luna Park, 1935

1 Luna Park

Luna Park has been a harbourside icon and favourite with Sydney children since the 1930s. Modelled on New York's Coney Island, this amusement park on the North Shore *(see p115)*, beside the Harbour Bridge, reopened in 2004 following major renovations. Enter through the 9-m (29.5-ft) clown face to enjoy classics such as the dodgems and the ferris wheel, and newer attractions such as the UFO. ✪ *Map D2 • 9922 6644*

2 Kids' Deck

The National Maritime Museum *(see p42)* runs Kids' Deck, a programme of creative activities for children aged 5 to 12. With events often linked to current exhibitions, kids might build their own ships or dress up. There are also regular activity sessions during school holidays and Mini Mariners sessions with story-times for pre-schoolers on Thursdays. ✪ *Kids' Deck: every Sun 11am–3pm • Adm*

3 Culture Vultures

The Art Gallery of New South Wales *(see p24–5)* has an extensive program of events for children of all ages. School holidays are peak times with special performances and workshops. There are kids' art classes once a month and Fundays on most Sundays, at 2:30pm, at which children might find themselves giggling at a mime artist or discovering Aboriginal art and culture.

4 Imax Theatre

The eight-storey-high screen and 15,000 watt digital surround sound system will have kids pinned to their seats, or jumping out of them, as the case may be. This Darling Harbour icon with the distinctive black-and-yellow chequerboard façade presents 2D and IMAX 3D films. State-of-the-art electronic headsets with infrared sensors have replaced the quaint 1950s cardboard glasses that parents might recall from their youth. ✪ *Map L4 • 9281 3300 • www.imax.com.au*

5 Circus Oz

Circus Oz mixes social commentary with satire, rock and roll, acrobatics and comedy to deliver performances that live up to their credo: Community, Diversity, Humanity, Hilarity.

Sign up for DK's email newsletter on traveldk.com

Horseriding at Centennial Park

They are a travelling troupe but usually perform at Sydney's Moore Park in January and February. Check out their website for performance dates. ❧ *Map E5 • www.circusoz.com*

6 Centennial Park
This parkland *(see p50)* has two main attractions for kids: a designated cycle path near Alison Road, and the Equestrian Centre on Lang and Robertson Roads *(see p54)*. The Centre runs tours for children and conducts hand-held pony rides. Centennial Park Cycles rents bikes and helmets for younger riders.

7 Kids at the House
This excellent program at the Sydney Opera House *(see pp8–11)* introduces children to the world of performance art. The Babies and Family proms acquaint kids aged two to nine with musical forms, often through interactive performances. Older children can enjoy Australian and international theatre at venues such as The Studio.

8 Storytime Readings
Children under five who fancy some downtime can attend Preschool Storytime sessions at the Balmain Library ❧ *Map C3*
• *Darling St, Balmain • 9367 9211*
• *Sessions: 11am Thu*

9 Fishing on the Harbour
One of the best spots to drop a line is at the Ives Steps Wharf, just under the Sydney Harbour Bridge west of Dawes Point Park *(see p13)*. This is a popular haunt for chatty older anglers who are happy to share their knowledge with children. ❧ *Map D2*
• *Ives Steps Wharf*

10 Discovering Nature and Culture
The Australian Museum *(see p42)* is the place for youngsters that are curious about the world around them. The museum offers unique tours, workshops and activities for children of all ages. Kids might take part in a mini dinosaur dig, get up close to spiders or explore the museum by torchlight after dark. Visit www.amonline.net.au for further information on child-centred activities at the museum.

Sydney's Child *is a free monthly magazine with tips for parents, available at bookstores and the Town Hall Information Centre.*

57

Left **Interior of Tetsuya's** Center **Wildfire interior** Right **Bondi Icebergs**

Restaurants

1 Tetsuya's
The emphasis of this serene space is on the food and wine. The dégustation *(see p141)* menus fuse Japanese flavours with French technique. Vegetarian dégustations are available on request. ◈ *Map M4 • 529 Kent St • 9267 2900 • Lunch Sat, dinner Tue–Sat • www.tetsuyas.com • $$$$$*

2 est.
This stylish spot is ideal for a luxurious meal. The Mod Oz menu boasts dishes such as crisp skin John Dory fillet on roasted Jerusalem artichokes. Don't miss the fabulous passion-fruit soufflé. ◈ *Map M2 • Level 1, Establishment Hotel, 252 George St • 9240 3010 • Lunch Mon–Fri, dinner Mon–Sat • Dis access • www.merivale.com/establishment • $$$*

Entrée at Wildfire

3 Guillaume at Bennelong
You can't beat dining at the Opera House *(see p9)*. Celebrity chef Guillaume Brahimi prepares Australian food with French skill. A less expensive option is to order tapas-style dishes from the cocktail bar. ◈ *9241 1999 • Lunch Thu–Fri, dinner Mon–Sat • www.guillaumeatbennelong.com.au • $$$$*

4 Wildfire
The glam Wildfire restaurant has an open kitchen, great for a big night out or a snack after a show. Enjoy a range of offerings from the wood-fired Brazilian *churrasco* grill, or pull up a seat at the Sea Bar for chilled seafood. Get one of Sydney's best cocktails at Ember, Wildfire's intimate bar. ◈ *Map M1 • Ground Level, Overseas Passenger Terminal, West Circular Quay • 8273 1222 • Lunch Mon–Fri, dinner Mon–Sun • Dis access • www.wildfire sydney.com • $$$*

5 Quay
Go for the views and for international flavours, especially in dishes such as butter poached murray cod and shaved sea scallops with smoked eel reduction. Tastes from France, Italy, Spain, Japan and China combine perfectly. ◈ *Map M1 • Overseas Passenger Terminal, Circular Quay • 9251 5600 • Lunch Tue–Fri, dinner daily • Dis access • www.quay.com.au • $$$$*

6 Icebergs Dining Room
This swish dining room is above the famous swimming pool *(see p49)*. Glamorous decor and modern Italian Mediterranean food. ◈ *Map H5 • 1 Notts Ave, Bondi Beach • 9365 9000 • Open Tue–Sun • www.idrb.com • $$$*

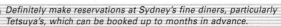

Guillaume at Bennelong

Definitely make reservations at Sydney's fine diners, particularly Tetsuya's, which can be booked up to months in advance.

Aria

7 Having deservedly regained its second hat Aria has confirmed its status as one of Sydeny's top restaurants with its elegant and inspired take on Mod Oz cuisine. The views over the harbour and Opera House are spectacular. A more reasonably priced, pre-theatre menu is available.

Aussie Wine

◈ Map D3 • 1 Macquarie St, Millers Point • 9252 2555 • Dis access • www.ariarestaurant.com.au • $$$

Otto Ristorante

8 A slice of Melbourne on the waterfront is so popular that it often draws celebrities to its handsome surrounds. The Italian fare is jazzed up with great local ingredients. ◈ Map P3 • Area 8, The Wharf, 6 Cowper Wharf Rd, Woolloomooloo • 9368 7488 • Dis access • www.ottoristorante.com.au • $$$

Longrain

9 Thai food lends itself well to sharing at Longrain, with dishes such as duck and potato curry with ginger and cucumber relish. Snack at the bar or sip offerings from the wine list. ◈ Map N5 • 85 Common-wealth St, Surry Hills • 9280 2888 • Lunch Mon–Fri, dinner Mon–Sun • Lunch bookings only • Dis access • www.longrain.com.au • $$

Sean's Panorama

10 Intimate and friendly, Sean's serves a small but lovely range of dishes such as linguine with shredded arugula, lemon and chilli and the famous white chocolate, fig and rosemary nougat. ◈ Map H5 • 270 Campbell Parade, Bondi Beach • 9365 4924 • Lunch Fri–Sun, dinner Wed–Sat • Optional BYO • Bookings essential • www.seanspanorama.com.au • $$$

Top 10 Seafood Highlights

1 Sydney Fish Market
The epicentre of all that's fishy in Sydney (see p105).

2 Rockpool
Star chef Neil Perry's seafood restaurant. ◈ Map M2 • 107 George St, The Rocks • 9252 1888

3 Flying Fish
Glam meets clams, with Mod Oz and Sri Lankan flavours. ◈ Map K3 • Jones Bay Wharf, 19–21 Pirrama Rd, Pyrmont • 9518 6677

4 Pier
Enjoy wonderful quality fish overlooking the harbour. ◈ Map G4 • 594 New South Head Rd, Rose Bay • 9327 6561

5 Coast
Very popular Darling Harbour spot. ◈ Map L4 • The Roof Terrace, Cockle Bay Wharf • 9267 6700

6 Manta Seafood
Great seafood in a beautiful marina setting. ◈ Map P3 • Wharf 9, 6 Cowper Wharf Rd, Woolloomooloo • 9332 3822

7 Fishface
Tiny but fab, serving the freshest fish. ◈ Map P5 • 132 Darlinghurst Rd • 9322 4803

8 A Fish Called Coogee
Get a feast from this seafood emporium. ◈ Map U5 • 229 Coogee Bay Rd, Coogee • 9664 7700

9 Mohr Fish
Popular fish and chips at a tiny but classy spot. ◈ Map D5 • 202 Devonshire St, Surry Hills • 9318 1326 • BYO

10 Garfish
The best fishy place on the north side also does great breakfast. ◈ Map D3 • 2/21 Broughton St, Kirribilli • 9922 4322 • Optional BYO

For more restaurants and a key to price categories see pp82, 89, 101, 107, 112, 119, 129.

Left **Museum of Sydney** Centre **Bill & Toni's** Right **Café Mint**

Casual Dining

1 Museum of Sydney Café

The food at a museum's café isn't normally a reason to visit, but this café is a treasure, serving breakfast, lunch and dinner to an appreciative crowd. Opening onto the paved forecourt, it offers excellent café standards such as sandwiches, salads and cakes, as well as bistro-style dishes such as steaks and tea-smoked trout. ※ Map N2 • Bridge & Phillip Sts • 9241 3636 • Open 7am–9pm Mon–Fri, 8:30am–5pm Sat–Sun • Dis access • $$

2 BBQ King

Despite its abrupt service and non-existent decor, this huge eatery has long held cult status. To understand why, try dining late after a big night on the town and you'll discover just how welcome this hearty food can be. Order the barbecued duck and Chinese beer. ※ Map M5 • 18–20 Goulburn St • 9267 2586 • Open 11:30am–2am daily • Optional BYO • $$

3 Pizza Mario

At this relocated restaurant, wood-fired, sparingly topped, thin and crusty pizzas are as close to the real thing as you will find in the inner city. The calzones are terrific, as is the fried calamari. ※ Map E4 • 417 Bourke St, Surry Hills • 9332 3633 • No booking • $

BBQ King in Chinatown

4 Bill & Toni's

This Sydney stalwart is loved for its strong coffee, free old-fashioned cordial and checked tablecloths. Upstairs, you'll find delicious home-style Italian, such as spaghetti Bolognese and bistecca. Head downstairs for gelato. ※ Map N5 • 74 Stanley St, East Sydney • 9360 4702 • Upstairs open noon–2:30pm & 6–10:30pm daily, downstairs open 7am–midnight daily • BYO • $

5 Billy Kwong

If the long queues aren't a dead give away, the delicious smells that greet you will make it clear that this place is special. Run by Kylie Kwong, Sydney's celebrity chef, Billy Kwong specializes in traditional Chinese family food souped up with a modern edge. ※ Map N6 • Shop 5, 355 Crown St, Surry Hills • 9332 3300 • Open 6–10pm Sun–Thu, 6–11pm Fri–Sat • Optional BYO • No bookings • $$

6 Bills Surry Hills

Really the best for breakfast but also great at other times, this restaurant is the showpiece of celebrity chef Bill Granger. At breakfast tuck into their speciality: delectable ricotta hotcakes with honeycomb butter and a sunrise juice. ※ Map N6 • 359 Crown St, Surry Hills • 9360 4762 • Open 7am–10pm daily • No bookings • Dis access • www.bills.com.au • $$

If you're craving fast food, try a Bondi burger from Oporto, a Portuguese chicken chain that has outlets all over Sydney.

7 Café Zoe

A light and airy room and pleasant service make this a good option. Eggs come with a choice of sides, the lunch menu contains great salads. Be sure to try an unusual fresh juice combo. ◎ *Map N6 • 688 Bourke St, Surry Hills • 8399 0940 • Open 7am–4pm Mon–Fri, 8am–4pm Sat • $*

8 Café Mint

The North African food at this small café is loaded with aromatic flavours such as cinnamon, mint and cumin. Try the varied *meze* plates with *dukkah*-coated Turkish bread. The big servings are great value. ◎ *Map N6 • 579 Crown St, Surry Hills • 9319 0848 • Open 7am–5pm Mon & Sat, 7am–11pm Tue–Fri • www.cafemint.com.au • $*

9 Marina Kiosk Rose Bay

Right on the water, this café is on the marina's wharf. Sit out in the sun or choose a shaded table. ◎ *Map G4 • 594 New South Head Rd • 9362 3555 • Open 8am–3:30pm Mon–Fri, 8am–4:30pm Sat–Sun • $*

10 The Bathers' Pavilion Café

Beachside at Balmoral *(see p48)*, this café is in the restored bathers' changerooms. The varied menu has great choices, and the ambience is wonderful. ◎ *Map U3 • 4 The Esplanade, Balmoral Beach • 9969 5050 • Open 7am–midnight daily • Dis access • No bookings • www.batherspavilion.com.au • $$*

The Bathers' Pavilion Café

Top 10 Breakfasts

1 Wall Café

Melbourne urban chic, scrumptious breakfasts and coffee. ◎ *Map D4 • 80 Campbell St, Surry Hills • 9280 1980*

2 Danks Street Depot

Try the creamed eggs at this fabulous café located in a gallery complex *(see p45)*. ◎ *9698 2201*

3 Lush on Bondi

Enjoy toasted wraps and uninterrupted views of the beach. ◎ *Map H5 • Queen Elizabeth Drive, Bondi Beach • 9300 8555.*

4 Brown Sugar

Groovy locals cosy in for big breakfasts and good coffee. ◎ *Map H4 • 106 Curlewis St, Bondi Beach • 9130 1566*

5 Caffe Salina

Hearty breakfasts with an Italian accent. ◎ *Map G6 • 479 Bronte Rd, Bronte • 9369 4012*

6 Blue Water Café

Soak up the view over breakfast. ◎ *Map U3 • 28 South Steyne, Manly • 9976 2051*

7 Corelli's Café

A bohemian vibe and large servings. ◎ *Map M3 • 325 King St, Newtown • 9550 4080*

8 Bourke Street Bakery

Gourmet tarts, sourdough breads and pasties, in or out. ◎ *Map N6 • 633 Bourke St, Surry Hills • 9699 1011*

9 Flat White

Try the sweet or savoury toast with fresh fluffy ricotta at this smart café. ◎ *Map F5 • Jersey Rd & Holdsworth St, Woollahra • 9328 9922*

10 Le Petit Crème

French café au laits and croque monsieurs. ◎ *Map P5 • Shop 2, 116–18 Darlinghurst Rd, Darlinghurst • 9361 4738*

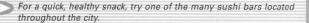

For a quick, healthy snack, try one of the many sushi bars located throughout the city.

Right **Leichhardt's Bar Italia** Centre **Dixon street entrance to Chinatown** Left **Lebanese baklava**

🔟 World Flavours

1 Italian

Leichhardt's thriving strip boasts a wonderful range of Italian food. The main section of Norton Street, running from its corner on Parramatta Road, is packed with cafés, bars and restaurants. Try the great pasta and gelato in the cheap and cheerful surroundings of Bar Italia. ⬈ *Map A4 • Bar Italia: 169–171 Norton St • 9560 9981*

2 Spanish

In a corner of the CBD you'll find the Torres Deli, selling chorizo and jamon, as well as several tapas joints. The Spanish Club serves yummy but lethal sangria. La Campana has Latin dance lessons on Wednesdays and Thursdays. ⬈ *Map M5 • Torres Deli: 75 Liverpool St • 9264 6862 • The Spanish Club: 88 Liverpool St • 9267 8440 La Campana: 53–55 Liverpool St • 9267 3787*

3 Japanese

A large Japanese community resides in the lower North Shore, and many good restaurants line Neutral Bay's Military Road. Sushi Studio (see p119) is the pick of them, but all offer authentic food, super-fresh sushi and good prices. To marvel at the unusual foods and amazing packaging of Japanese groceries, visit Anegawa Enterprises Pty Ltd. ⬈ *Map D1 • Anegawa: 7 Waters Rd • 9904 4177*

Fresh sushi

4 Cantonese

Excellent Cantonese food can be found all over Sydney, but head to Chinatown (see p82) for the widest selection. The market on Dixon Street makes it particularly lively on Friday nights. Browsing the arcades off the Dixon Street Mall often leads to interesting discoveries such as herbal remedies, dried fish snacks and jade carvings. ⬈ *Map M5*

5 Turkish

Catch a train into Auburn and it's a short stroll to the heart of the Turkish community. Try kebabs and *pide*, Turkish pizza, at Sofra. Finish up with a thick Turkish coffee and dondurma, traditional ice cream made from *salep* (orchid tubers) at Mado. ⬈ *Map S4 • Al Sofra: 35–39 Auburn Rd • 9649 9167 • Mado: 63 Auburn Rd • 9643 5299*

6 Portuguese

Portuguese custard tarts, *natas*, are found all over Sydney, but you haven't really tasted them until you've tried Honeymoon Patisserie. Silvas offers traditional charcoal chicken and Gloria's Café serves up great country dishes. ⬈ *Map A5 • Honeymoon Patisserie: 96 New Canterbury Rd, Petersham • 9564 2389 • Silvas: 82–86 New Canterbury Rd • 9572 9911 • Gloria's Café: 82 Audley St • 9568 3966*

Thai restaurants are on almost every Sydney corner. The food is fresh and tasty but be careful if you can't handle spices.

7 Lebanese

The central Lebanese mosque is at Lakemba but the best food can be found at the suburb of Punchbowl. Head to The Boulevarde for hummus, falafel and baklava. Jasmin1 is a good place for a very quick, cheap and tasty meal. Nearby Summerland is a bit more swish and has bellydancers most nights. ⬡ Map S5 • Jasmin1: 224 The Boulevarde • 9740 7866 • Summerland: 457 Chappel Rd, Bankstown • 9708 5107

8 Kosher

Any kind of food could be kosher, but two main styles, Israeli and traditional Jewish food, are readily available in the Bondi area. Savion is the stalwart, offering Israeli street food such as chicken shwarmas. Try Katzy's for chicken soup with matza balls, and don't miss the bagels and cakes at Carmel Bakery. ⬡ Map Q5 • Savion: 38 Wairoa Ave • 9130 6357 Katzy's: 113 Hall St • 9130 6755 • Carmel: • 175 Oxford St Mall, Bondi Jct • 9386 0999

9 Greek

While there are many Greek businesses in Marrickville and it's fun to browse the many shops on Marrickville Road, the best Greek restaurants are spread further out. For wonderful modern food, visit Perama. Steki Taverna is more traditional, plate-smashing included. ⬡ Map A5 • Perama: 88 Audley St, Petersham • 9569 7534 • Steki Taverna: 2 O'Connell St, Newtown • 9516 2191

10 Indian

Many of Sydney's Indian community choose to eat at the authentic restaurants in Surry Hills, several of which are packed into a small section of Cleveland Street between Crown and Bourke Streets. Have a South Indian flavoured thali or masala dosa at the vegetarian restaurant Maya, and then sample some of the traditional sweets. The neighbouring shops sell Indian ingredients, spices, incense, and Bollywood movies. ⬡ Map D5 • Maya: 470 Cleveland St • 9699 8663

Indian Sweets

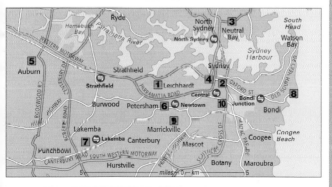

About 31% of Sydneysiders were born overseas and over 900,000 people speak a language other than English at home.

63

Left **Opera House** Centre **Bangarra Dance Theatre** Right **Sydney Theatre Company** poster

🔟 Performing Arts Companies

1 Opera Australia
Experience the energy and passion of the national opera company when the young singers and international stars of Opera Australia perform at the Sydney Opera House *(see pp8–11)* from January to April and June to November. ☎ 9318 8200 • *www.opera-australia.org.au*

2 Sydney Symphony
Also a resident of the Opera House, the Sydney Symphony performs in the spectacular concert hall. The orchestra performances range from jazz and film soundtracks to classical orchestral masterpieces with the world's most illustrious conductors and soloists. ☎ 8215 4600 • *www.sydneysymphony.com*

3 Sydney Theatre Company
Performing regularly at the Sydney Theatre at Walsh Bay *(see p46)*, Sydney's premier theatre company are also in residence at the Sydney Opera House as well as performing at their home theatre at the Wharf under the Sydney Harbour Bridge. The STC presents an exciting mix of classics and new Australian drama. ☎ *Map M1 •* 9250 1777 • *www.sydneytheatre.com.au*

4 Sydney Dance Company
With acclaimed dancers and guest choreographers, Sydney Dance Company has paved the way for the development of Australia's fun-loving dance scene. The studio also runs daily dance classes for jazz, hip-hop and ballet, after which you can feast in the Sydney Dance Café, which has views of the Sydney Harbour Bridge. ☎ 9221 4811 • *www.sydneydancecompany.com*

5 Bangarra Dance Theatre
This unique company blends traditional Aboriginal and Torres Strait Islander history and culture with international contemporary dance. Powerful, startling and inherently spiritual, Bangarra speaks with an ancient yet completely modern voice. ☎ 9251 5333 • *www.bangarra.com.au*

6 Australian Chamber Orchestra
Daring programming and stylistic versatility set this chamber orchestra apart – and the fact that the violinists play standing up. The players have a sense of cohesion usually only found in smaller ensembles. ☎ 8274 3800 • *www.aco.com.au*

Australian Chamber Orchestra

Buy tickets from Ticketek: 132 849; www.ticketek.com.au

Bell Shakespeare

7 Witness Shakespeare like you've never seen. Since its foundation in 1990 by John Bell and Anna Volska, Sydney's theatrical blue-bloods, this company has presented the works of the Bard and modern classics in an accessible style. ✆ 8298 9000 • www.bellshakespeare.com.au

Company B

8 Housed in the historic Belvoir St Theatre, Company B deserves its great reputation for producing sharp contemporary theatre. Its edgy shows are always popular, particularly with the young, hip crowd, so get in early for tickets. Landmark productions have included Cloudstreet, Toy Symphony, The Alchemist, The Small Poppies, Exit the King and Stuff Happens. ✆ Map M6 • 9699 3444 • www.belvoir.com.au

Ensemble Theatre

9 Australia's longest continuously running professional theatre is located in a converted boatshed on Careening Cove. The company performs a mix of local and international plays with an emphasis on ensemble values. Reliable and definitely rewarding. ✆ Map D2 • 9929 0644 • www.ensemble.com.au

Australian Theatre for Young People

10 Australia's flagship youth theatre company presents radical versions of classics, plays by young writers, physical theatre and works written by leading Australian writers, such as Louis Nowra and Debra Oswald. Many up-and-coming stars got their first taste of the limelight here. Nicole Kidman is one of its celebrity patrons. ✆ 9251 3900 • www.atyp.com.au

Top 10 Sydney Celebrities

1 Nicole Kidman
The famous Australian actress lives in her new Walsh Bay penthouse for at least part of the year.

2 Russell Crowe
From a penthouse atop the Woolloomooloo Finger Bay Wharf, the star of *Master and Commander* continues to enjoy water views.

3 Dame Joan Sutherland
Opera diva Joan Sutherland has lived in Potts Point for much of her long and prestigious career.

4 Toni Collette
A daring lead performance in *Muriel's Wedding* launched Collette on the world stage; she lives in Tamarama.

5 Ben Lee
Former Noise Addict, now solo strummer, Lee beds down at Bondi when he isn't hanging out in New York.

6 Megan Gale
A supermodel in Italy, Gale often returns to Sydney to hit the runways.

7 Judy Davis
One of Australia's most respected actors, Davis has taken some of film's top honours; she lives in Balmain.

8 David Wenham
The critically-acclaimed actor is at home in Sydney's Eastern Suburbs.

9 Hugo Weaving
Despite roles in *The Matrix* and *The Lord of the Rings*, the modest Weaving still calls Sydney home.

10 Bryan Brown
The iconic Aussie actor is often seen on Sydney's northern beaches.

The Australian Chamber Orchestra performs regularly at the City Recital Hall

🔟 Nightlife & Live Music

1 Metro Theatre

Tiered levels rising to the bar at the back of the main room mean you can see the stage from anywhere in the room. That, plus great acoustics, makes this one of Sydney's best live music venues. 🕲 *Map M2 • 624 George St • 9550 3666 • www. metrotheatre.com.au*

2 City Recital Hall

The first specifically-designed concert venue built in Sydney since the Opera House, the 1973 City Recital Hall is an uplifting space, ideal for acoustic music. The quality of sound has already attracted Australia's leading companies, including the Australian Chamber Orchestra, Musica Viva and the Sydney Philharmonic Choir.
🕲 *Map M3 • Angel Place • 8256 2222 • www. cityrecitalhall.com.au*

3 Home

There's no place like Home. Since its opening night performance by Paul Oakenfold, Sydney's only true superclub has been packed solid. The massive club features a multi-levelled main room, a chill-out zone, the infamous padded "Box" and an outdoor terrace.

Also attached is Homebar, a casual café and mellow bar. The hottest Sydney DJs have residencies here, and top international acts are regularly featured. 🕲 *Map L4 • Cockle Bay Wharf, Darling Park • 9266 0600 • www.homesydney.com*

4 The Basement

A landmark of the Australian jazz, blues and roots scene since the early 1970s, the walls of The Basement are covered in autographed photos of the stars who have graced its stage. The venue boasts live music every night of the week, and both dinner-and-showpackages or standing tickets are available to buy. 🕲 *Map M2 • 29 Reiby Place, Circular Quay • 9251 2797 • www. thebasement.com.au*

5 The Cat & Fiddle Hotel

Sydney's hardest-working live venue hosts more than 30 bands and solo artists every week, so there's music to suit every taste. This musician-friendly bar has a strong local follow-ing, particularly for their Sunday after-noon sessions.
🕲 *Map K1 • 456 Darling St, Balmain • 9810 7931 • www. thecatandfiddle.net*

Sign for The Cat & Fiddle Hotel

Pick up a copy of free weekly music newspaper The Drum Media for gig listings, or 3D World for club and dance listings.

Rock band Fur Patrol at the Annandale Hotel

Annandale Hotel
This legendary Sydney live venue is a must-visit for anyone interested in the local music scene. The pub hosts live music most nights of the week, featuring everyone from local stalwarts to smaller international acts. If you get peckish, step out back for healthy Thai-Asian inspired food at Annandale's Wok & Roll, a laid back local eat-in and take-away spot. ⊗ Map B5 • Parramatta Rd & Nelson St, Annandale • 0550 1070 • www.annandalehotel.com

Selinas at Coogee Bay Hotel
Selinas marks the revival of a once-mighty live venue. This spot caters to devotees of Oz Rock and those who don't mind their ears ringing the next day. It's located in the backpacker haven of The Coogee Bay Hotel, which accommodates six bars. ⊗ Map U4 • Coogee Bay Rd & Arden St • 9005 0000 • www.coogeebayhotel.com.au

The Vanguard
This Newtown venue specializes in jazz, blues and roots music. Bands play Tuesday to Sunday, and you're likely to hear anything from Latin jazz to country soul on their eclectic bill. The non-smoking venue also features a cocktail bar and offers dinner-and-show packages. ⊗ Map B5 • 42 King St, Newtown • 9557 7992 • www.thevanguard.com.au

The Hopetoun Hotel
This tiny venue packs them in for live music seven nights a week. The mostly local acts run from alternative rock and pop to country. The atmosphere is friendly and the room looks more like a lounge than a bar. ⊗ Map N6 • 416 Bourke St, Surry Hills • 9361 5257 • www.myspace.com/hopetoun

Tank
The central element at this nightclub is the music, and the main dance floor pumps with pure house. Rehydrate at one of three bars or relax and soak up the atmosphere. The decor is a throwback to Studio 54. ⊗ Map M2 • 3 Bridge Lane • 8295 9960 • www.tankclub.com.au

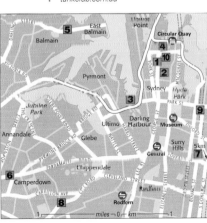

The Drum Media and 3D World newspapers are available at most record shops and venues.

Left **Jetty Bar at the Manly Wharf Hotel** Right **Opera Bar**

Pubs & Bars

1 Opera Bar

Views don't come much better than the Opera Bar's *(see p9)* panorama of the harbour, Harbour Bridge and city skyline. Soak up the sun on the terrace during the day, or sip cocktails in the evening. A good bar menu means you can make a night of it, adding to the perfect Sydney experience. ® *Lower Concourse, Sydney Opera House • 9247 1666 • Open 11:30am–late daily • www.operabar.com.au*

2 Cruise

Cruise offers great views of the Opera House. Modern and stylish, the glowing feature wall of this bar periodically changes in colour and mood. A chic crowd makes up for the slightly haphazard service. ® *Map M2 • Level 1, Overseas Passenger Terminal, West Circular Quay • 9251 1188 • Open 11am–late daily*

3 Establishment

Resurrected from the burnt-out shell of an 1892 emporium, this hotel boasts a 42-m (138-ft) marble bar and designer fit-out. It's very civilised mid-week, but by Friday it's packed with the after-work crowd. There are seating areas where you can escape the hordes. Upstairs, the exotic Hemmesphere bar specialises in mojitos. ® *Map M2 • 252 George St • 9240 3000 • Open 11am–late Mon–Fri, 6pm–late Sat*

4 Arthouse Hotel

This groovy city hangout boasts four bars and a restaurant over three levels. The main bar, The Verge, was once a chapel and features 19th-century stencilling and skylights. The Dome lounge and Attic bar provide more intimate surrounds, and on Saturday nights the Gallery bar on the ground floor transforms into KINK, featuring local and international DJs. There is also a programme of performances and special events, and permanent art installations. ® *Map M4 • 275 Pitt St • 9284 1200 • Open 11am–late Mon–Fri, 5pm–6am Sat • www.thearthousehotel. com.au*

5 The Loft

This hip bar brings style to Darling Harbour. Spectacular views and good service make it a winner. Tapas-style snacks are available till 10pm. ® *Map L3 • King Street Wharf, 3 Lime St • 9299 4770 • Open 4pm–1am Mon–Wed, 4pm–3am Thu, noon–3am Fri–Sat, noon–1am Sun • www.theloftsydney.com*

6 The Tilbury

This once-grungy dive has been revamped as a stylish bar and Italian restaurant. A DJ plays at the bar Friday and Saturday, and Sunday afternoons feature live jazz at the restaurant. ® *Map P3 • 12–18 Nicholson St, Woolloomooloo • 9368 1955 • Open 7am–midnight Mon–Fri, 9am–midnight Sat, 10am–10pm Sun*

Toohey's Bitter

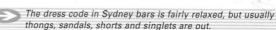

The dress code in Sydney bars is fairly relaxed, but usually thongs, sandals, shorts and singlets are out.

7 Manly Wharf Hotel

If the large public bar with its communal tables and lively atmosphere is too hectic for you, head outdoors to the Jetty Bar to watch the sun set over the harbour, or hide away in the cocktail lounge. Fireplaces provide cosy winter warmth. ◈ Map U3 • Manly Wharf East Esplanade, Manly • 9977 1266 • Open 11:30am–midnight Mon–Fri, 11am–midnight Sat, 11am–10pm Sun • www.manlywharfhotel.com.au

8 Darlo Bar

A hip local hangout with a relaxed 1950s and 60s decor. Close to the Victoria and Oxford Street restaurants, it's a good place to meet for a drink. Grab a drop from the bottle shop before leaving. ◈ Map P5 • 306 Liverpool St, Darlinghurst • 9331 3672 • Open 10am–midnight Mon–Sat, noon–midnight Sun

9 Ravesi's

The fold-back glass doors at the ever-crowded Ravesi's allow the party to spill out onto the street. It's a great place for a cocktail, but conversation can prove difficult when the local crowds get loud. ◈ Map I15 • 110 Campbell Parade, Bondi Beach • 9365 4422 • Open 10am–1am Mon–Sat, 10am–midnight Sun • www.ravesis.com.au

10 Bondi Icebergs

You don't have to take an icy dip in the famous pool to have a true Icebergs experience. Simply watch a Bondi sunset over a beer in the low-key Icebergs Club (see p35) and you're taking part in a great local tradition. If you're feeling glam and your wallet can take the strain, don't miss the stylish bar attached to the Icebergs Dining Room (see p58). ◈ 1 Notts Ave, Bondi • 9130 3120 • Open 10am–1pm Mon–Thu, 10am–midnight Fri–Sat, 9am–11pm Sun • www.icebergs.com.au

Top 10 Late-Night Haunts

1 Wildfire

A great place to head after a concert. The kitchen is open until 1am on Fridays and Saturdays (see p58).

2 BBQ King

Fast, cheap, unfussy Chinese food and famous Peking Duck 'til 2am (see p60).

3 The Victoria Room

Melbourne meets the Med. ◈ Map E4 • 235 Victoria St, Darlinghurst • 9357 4488

4 Bar Cleveland

Trendy but unpretentious, open 'til the small hours. ◈ Map D5 • Bourke & Cleveland Sts, Surry Hills • 9698 1908

5 Mars Lounge

Music and fine cocktails until late in this chic bar. ◈ Map M5 • 16 Wentworth Ave, Surry Hills • 9267 6440

6 Civic Hotel

This Art Deco pub runs 'til 6am Fridays and Saturdays. ◈ Map M4 • 388 Pitt St • 8080 7000

7 Town Hall Hotel

This legendary hangout doesn't even fire up until midnight. ◈ Map B5 • 326 King St, Newtown • 9557 1206

8 Maisve

Tasty snacks and light meals at this 24-hour café. ◈ Map D1 • 164 Military Rd, Neutral Bay • 9908 4030

9 Café Hernandez

Open 24 hours for coffee and Spanish treats with the poets, artists and musos. ◈ Map P5 • 60 Kings Cross Rd, Potts Point • 9331 2343

10 Baron's

This night-owl haunt is full of faded glamour. Open until 6am. ◈ Map Q4 • 5 Roslyn St, Kings Cross • 9358 6131

In Australia, pubs and bars are commonly known as "hotels".

Left **The Bookshop Darlinghurst** Right **Public bar at the Imperial Hotel**

Gay & Lesbian Friendly Places

1 Oxford Street Shops

Called the Golden Mile, the stretch of Oxford Street *(see p92)* between Taylor Square and Hyde Park has long been home to gay and lesbian bars, clubs and shops. Each February the Mardi Gras parade *(see p72)* passes this route. Check out Aussie Boys for Sydney Speedos and the Grumpy Baker for a snack and coffee.

Bank Hotel façade

2 The Colombian

The best of the Oxford Street bars is a mock Central American jungle. Giant windows open to the street, allowing the Colombian to serve up people-watching with the beer. The crowd is a mixed bunch of gay, lesbian and straight, and after sundown the vibe turns from relaxed afternoon drinks to a party. ◈ *Map N5 • Corner of Oxford & Crown Sts, Surry Hills • 9360 2151 • Open late daily*

3 Green Park Hotel

A good spot for those who'd rather avoid a mainstream gay bar, this pub attracts a trendy Darlinghurst crowd. On Sundays it's packed with those recovering from their weekends with a beer and game of pool. ◈ *Map P5 • 360 Victoria St, Darlinghurst • 9380 5311 • Open 10am–2am Mon–Sat, noon–midnight Sun*

4 The Bank Hotel

This popular Newtown pub underwent a major make over but survived with its character intact. The cocktail bar and Thai restaurant are as packed and boisterous as ever. ◈ *Map B5 • 324 King St, Newtown • 8568 1900 • Open noon–late daily • www.bankhotel.com.au*

5 Manacle

Apart from hosting regular nights, this gay and lesbian bar specialises in fetish theme nights, encouraging patrons to don their uniform, rubber, leather or bike gear. All men and women are welcome. Fetish gear is not essential. A 24-hour license holder, this place has a capacity for around 350 guests and there are several sections. ◈ *Map A5 • Clarence Hotel, 450 Parramatta Rd, Petersham • 9560 0400 • www.clarencehotel.com.au*

6 Imperial Hotel

Some of the classic drag show venues have closed down, but this stalwart is still going strong. The hotel was featured in the cult film *Priscilla, Queen of the Desert*. There are shows at the Imperial most nights, so call ahead to find out events and times. ◈ *Map C6 • 35 Erskineville Rd, Erskineville • 9519 9899 • www.theimperialhotel.com.au*

Pick up the weekly Sydney Star Observer *and monthly magazine* Lesbians On The Loose *to find out what's happening in Sydney.*

7 The Bookshop Darlinghurst

All kinds of queer fiction are packed into this great shop, which covers everything from photography tomes to contemporary lesbian fiction and life-style books. ◈ Map N5 • 207 Oxford St, Darlinghurst • 9331 1103 • Open 10am–10pm Mon–Wed, 10am–11pm Thu, 10am–midnight Fri–Sat, 11am–11pm Sun • www.thebookshop.com.au

8 Ginseng Bathhouse

These traditional Korean baths have separate male and female facilities that include steam rooms, saunas, hot baths and the famous ginseng baths. Soak in the soothing waters or get a skin scrub and massage. ◈ Map P4 • Level 1, 224 Victoria St, Potts Point • 9356 3477 • Open 9:30am–9:30pm Mon–Fri, 9am–9:30pm Sat–Sun • Adm • www.ginsengbathhouse.com.au

9 Café Lounge

This laidback courtyard café is patronised by art school kids and grungy types. Arty ambience with comfy sofas, good coffee, and vegetarian options such as tofu and juices. ◈ Map N5 • 277 Gouldburn St, Surry Hills • Open 5pm–10:30pm Tue–Thu, 11:30am–midnight Fri, 9am–midnight Sat, 9am–9pm Sun • 9356 8888 • www.cafelounge.com.au

10 Ken's at Kensington

Sydney's original gay sauna and gym offers an indoor swimming pool, weights area, spa and steam room. There are also video and coffee lounges, towel-free nights and a DJ on weekends. Only men are allowed at Ken's at Kensington. ◈ Map E6 • 83 Anzac Parade, Kensington • 9662 1359 • Open 11–8am Mon–Thu, 11–6am Fri–Mon (non-stop) • Adm • www.kensatkensington.com.au

Top 10 Mardi Gras Events

1 Festival
A month-long arts and cultural festival with dance parties, performing arts, community and sports events.

2 Parade
Thousands attend the notorious Mardi Gras parade, the finale of the festival.

3 Party
Held after the parade, this is one of the largest and most spectacular gay dance parties.

4 Fair Day
Features stalls, music, food and "Kid's Zone", an area that offers a range of activities for children and their families.

5 Mardi Gras Film Festival
A great collection of global queer cinema is screened over two weeks. ◈ www.queerscreen.com.au

6 History Walks
"The Sisters of Perpetual Indulgence" present hilarious walking tours of Toronga Zoo and other sites across Sydney

7 Shop Yourself Stupid
The largest shopping day in the gay and lesbian calendar offers an array of attractions and specials.

8 Hats Off
A gala night of music, entertainment and celebrities to raise money for HIV/AIDS charities. ◈ 9360 5557 • www.acon.com.au

9 Bike & Tattoo Show
The "Dykes on Bikes" present entertainment, games, bikes and tattoos for your viewing pleasure.

10 Team Sydney
Various sporting events, competitions and games. ◈ www.teamsydney.org.au

Information about the annual Mardi Gras Festival and surrounding events can be found at www.mardigras.org.au

Left **Gay & Lesbian Mardi Gras** Right **Sydney to Hobart Yacht Race**

🔟 Festivals & Events

1 Sydney Festival
Time your visit to coincide with this month-long international extravaganza of music, theatre, visual arts, dance and more. Past performers have included Michael Nyman, the London Sinfonietta, the Kronos Quartet, the Russian National Orchestra, the Steppenwolf Theatre Company, Vietnamese Water Puppets and Les Ballets Africains. 🔊 *Jan • www.sydneyfestival.org.au*

2 Big Day Out
This rock-and-roll road show began in the early 1990s. Today, international acts mix it up with alternative and popular local outfits. In recent years bands have included Silverchair, Metallica, Paul Kelly, The Magic Numbers, PJ Harvey and Kraftwerk. 🔊 *Jan/Feb • Sydney Showgrounds • www.bigdayout.com*

3 Australia Day
Celebrating the arrival of Sydney's First Fleet, this national holiday sees Sydney ferries and Tall Ships competing in the big race from the Harbour Bridge to Manly and back. There are free concerts and performances held across the city. Do keep in mind that to many indigenous people, this date is known as "Invasion Day". 🔊 *26 Jan • www.australiaday.com.au*

4 Gay & Lesbian Mardi Gras
This carnival is more than just a street parade down Oxford Street *(see p92)*, for more than a quarter-million people line the route. The parade naturally ends with a party, but there is also an energetic programme of associated events that celebrates the strength and diversity of gay Sydney *(see pp70–71)*. 🔊 *Feb or Mar • www.mardigras.org.au*

5 Sydney Writers' Festival
The roll-call at this week-long event includes more than 200 international and local speakers, with the odd Nobel Laureate thrown in for good measure. There are panel discussions, master classes, book launches and readings aplenty. And the festival caters to all tastes, from sci-fi to romance. 🔊 *May • www.swf.org.au*

6 NAIDOC Week
The Australia-wide National Aborigines and Islanders Day Observance Committee Week celebrates the survival, diversity and strength of Torres Strait Islander and Aboriginal cultures. Themes change annually, but regular events include a prestigious art award and prizes in a variety of categories ranging from sports to community leadership. 🔊 *Early Jul • www.naidoc.org.au*

Tall Ship on Australia Day

7 Rugby League Grand Final
Although Australian Rules Football is catching on in Sydney, the locals still go nuts when the big fellas from Sydney's professional league battle it out at Sydney Stadium. If you can't book a ticket, catch the action at your local pub. ✆ Sep

8 Festival of the Winds
Ever since Hargrave took to the sky with four box kites (see p31), Sydneysiders have loved their kites. And there's no better venue for a day of mass kiting than Bondi Beach (see pp34–5), site of Australia's largest kite-flying festival. Highlights include live music, dance shows, food stalls and workshops. ✆ Sep • www.waverley.nsw.gov.au/info/pavillion/fotw

9 Manly International Jazz Festival
Australia's largest community-based celebration of jazz in all its forms, from trad to bebop, has been running for 30 years. Manly (see p118) gives itself over to jazz for the Labour Day long weekend. In addition to travelling bands, there are performances held at outdoor venues such as the ocean beachfront, and indoor venues such as St. Mathews Church on The Corso. ✆ Oct • www.manly.nsw.gov.au/manlyjazz

10 Sydney to Hobart Yacht Race
Organized by the Cruising Yacht Club of Australia, this blue-water classic has been Australia's best known yacht race for over half a century. Crowds line the harbour to wave off the crews as they pass through The Heads (see p51) and head down the coast to Tasmania, almost 628 nautical miles south. ✆ 26 Dec, Boxing Day • rolexsydneyhobart.com

Top 10 Film Festivals

1 Sydney Film Festival
Watch films all day, everyday, for 2 weeks. ✆ Jun • www.sydneyfilmfestival.org

2 Mardi Gras Film Festival
Screens worldwide gay cinema and camp classics (see p71). ✆ Feb or March • www.queerscreen.com.au

3 Tropfest
The biggest short film festival in the world screens outdoors at the Domain. ✆ Feb • www.tropfest.com

4 Italian Film Festival
Classic and contemporary cinema. ✆ Oct • www.italianfilmfestival.com.au

5 Festival of German Cinema
A mix of dramas, docos, shorts and cult movies. ✆ Apr • www.goethe.de/australia

6 Japanese Film Festival
The Japan Foundation, Sydney – Cultural Section organizes international guests and retrospectives. ✆ Nov • www.jpf.org.au

7 Alliance Française French Film Festival
Presents the latest, most stylish and provocative in French cinema. ✆ Mar • www.frenchfilmfestival.org

8 Spanish Film Festival
Often very cheeky, always great fun. ✆ May • www.spanishfilmfestival.com

9 Australian Festival of Jewish Cinema
Diverse Jewish films from around the globe. ✆ Nov

10 Flickerfest
Australia's only competitive international short film festival. ✆ Jan • www.flickerfest.com.au

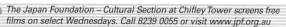

The Japan Foundation – Cultural Section at Chifley Tower screens free films on select Wednesdays. Call 8239 0055 or visit www.jpf.org.au

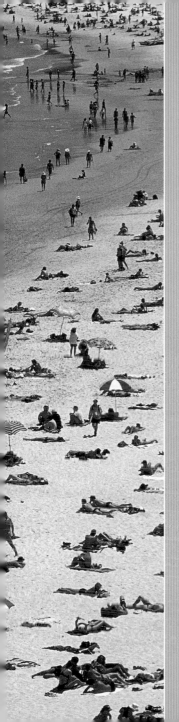

AROUND TOWN

SYDNEY'S TOP 10

Left **State Theatre interior** Centre **Statues on Anzac Memorial** Right **Sydney Tower Deck**

City Centre

SYDNEYSIDERS WORK HARD AND PLAY HARD. *And there's no better place to see them in action than the city centre, which is a manic tide of shoppers, opinionated taxi drivers, feral bicycle couriers and office workers talking furiously into their mobile phones as they power-walk to their next appointment. The city centre is surrounded by Circular Quay, The Rocks, the Botanic Gardens, the Domain, Central Station, Darling Harbour and Chinatown. Within this precinct you'll find historic sites and buildings sandwiched between chi-chi boutiques, groovy bars and restaurants, elegant Victorian shopping arcades and a host of entertainment venues. While it's easy to get caught up in the flow, don't forget to stop every once in a while to enjoy the architecture or the numerous street performers.*

View of the harbour from Sydney Tower

Sights

1. Museum of Sydney
2. Martin Place
3. St Mary's Cathedral
4. Sydney Tower
5. Strand Arcade
6. State Theatre
7. Anzac Memorial
8. Queen Victoria Building
9. Town Hall
10. St Andrew's Cathedral

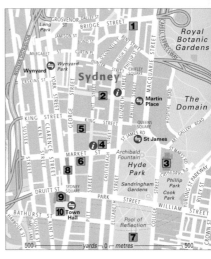

Previous pages: **Bondi Beach**

Left **Entrance to the Museum of Sydney** Right **Martin Place**

Museum of Sydney

This stunning museum *(see p42)* occupies the site of Australia's first Government House, a prefabricated structure that was shipped over with the First Fleet in 1788. That structure was demolished in 1846, but some of its original footings are still visible through glass panels set into the floor. The museum places the history of white settlement against the Aboriginal custodianship of the land. The museum's plaza features *Edge of the Trees (see p47)*, an installation and soundscape which explores Aboriginal history and culture.

Martin Place

Martin Place runs from the General Post Office on George Street uphill to Macquarie Street. The 1891 GPO was designed by James Barnet *(see p85)* and built over the Tank Stream *(see p18)*. Check out the amusing characters above the Pitt Street colonnade *(see walk, p79)* and the grand 1912 Commonwealth Bank Head Office. The bank's equally impressive 1928 sibling resides just up the hill. Opposite the GPO is the striking 1925 Neo-Classical National Australia Bank, and the Cenotaph commemorating Australia's war heroes. ◎ *Map N3*

Cenotaph at Martin Place

St Mary's Cathedral

One of the world's largest Gothic Revival churches, the original 1833 structure of this cathedral was destroyed by a fire in 1865. Its replacement was designed by William Wardell and work began on it the same year. The twin spires, which featured in Wardell's original plans, were only completed in 2000. The design of the magnificent terrazzo floor in the crypt is based on the Story of Creation and the *Book of Kells*; it took 15 years to complete. ◎ *Map N4* • *9220 0400* • *Worship only; Mass on Sunday*

Sydney Tower

This 305-m (1,000-ft) icon offers 360-degree views over the Sydney region. The turret has revolving restaurants, a coffee shop and an observation deck. Above this is a 162,000-litre (35,500-gallon) water tank that acts as a stabilizer on windy days. The tower offers two attractions – Skywalk, an adrenaline-filled 45-minute guided walk around the roof with incredible views of the city and OzTrek, a virtual reality ride across Australia with 180-degree cinema screens, 3D holographic imagery and real-motion seating. ◎ *Map M4* • *Podium Level, 100 Market St* • *9333 9222* • *Tower & OzTrek: 9am–10:30pm daily (to 11:30pm Sat)* • *Skywalk: 9am–10pm daily* • *Adm*

Queen Victoria's Dog
A statue of Queen Victoria and a wishing well stand at the QVB's main entrance. As you approach, a recorded voice recounts the story of Queen Victoria's favourite terrier, Islay, who was "granted the power of speech" for helping deaf and blind children. And what a voice! Islay's story is told by none other than Sydney's "Golden Tonsils", radio shock-jock John Laws.

Strand Arcade
Although Melbournians will disagree, this may be Australia's most impressive Victorian-era glass-roofed shopping arcade. Designed by John Spencer and opened in 1892, this quiet and elegant arcade (see p80) is home to boutiques, jewellers, tailors, coffee shops and groovy home-ware stores such as Funkis and Dinosaur Designs (see p81). Pressed-metal stairs and quaint lifts service the three levels and there is a seating area at the western end of the upper levels where you can enjoy a cup of tea overlooking the shoppers below. ✪ Map M3 • 412–414 George St • 9232 4199 • www.strandarcade.com.au

Strand Arcade

Baroque foyer of the State Theatre

State Theatre
Originally a cinema with over-the-top Gothic, Baroque and Art Deco elements, this 1929 National Trust-classified "Palace of Dreams" was designed by Henry White, who also worked on the Capitol Theatre (see p29). Sweeping staircases embrace its lavish Grand Assembly foyer, and the massive 20,000-piece Koh-i-Nor chandelier dominates the 2,000-seat auditorium. Since 1974, this theatre has been the premier venue for the Sydney Film Festival (see p73). During the year it presents live acts and musical performances, which have included Bette Midler and kd lang. ✪ Map M4 • 49 Market St • 9373 6655 • www.statetheatre.com.au • Guided tours, call to book • Adm

Anzac Memorial
Mirrored in Hyde Park's Pool of Reflection is this 1934 Art Deco monument built to

Anzac Memorial

commemorate Australia's WWI dead (see p36). It now records the sacrifices made by thousands of Australians in subsequent conflicts. The Hall of Memory is on the upper level, overlooking Raynor Hoff's moving statue, and the Hall of Silence is on the ground floor. A small museum on the ground floor features photographs and artifacts. ✪ Map N5 • Hyde Park: 9267 7668 • Open 9am–5pm daily

Façade of the Queen Victoria Building

8 Queen Victoria Building
The four-storey Romanesque QVB *(see p80)* staggers visitors with its beautiful tiled floors, elegant staircases, stained glass, barrel-vaulted glass ceiling and copper domed roof. Built on the site of the old Sydney markets, this landmark was designed by George McRae and opened to applause in 1898. Today, the QVB houses local and international fashion brands. ◈ *Map M4*

9 Town Hall
John Henry Wilson originally designed Sydney's civic headquarters in 1868. The front steps of this Victorian building, with its 1884 clock tower, elegant 1877 vestibule and grand 1889 Centennial Hall, have been a favourite meeting place for Sydneysiders since the original *porte cochère* facing George Street was removed in 1934. ◈ *Map M4 • 9265 9189 • Open 8am–6pm Mon–Fri*

10 St Andrew's Cathedral
Australia's oldest Gothic Revival cathedral was designed in 1868 by Edmund Blaket, who also designed St Stephen's *(see p103)*. It contains many memorials to Sydney pioneers, such as the 19th-century merchant-prince Thomas Mort, a major figure in the history of Sydney's harbour. ◈ *Map M4 • Sydney Square • 9265 1661 Open 10am–4pm Mon–Sat, 8am–8pm Sun • Tours available*

A Walk from Circular Quay to the QVB

Morning

From **Circular Quay** *(see p18)* follow Loftus Street to **Macquarie Park**, exhibiting the anchor from the First Fleet HMS *Sirius*. Across the road is the 1876 **Lands Department Building**, seat of early European land ownership. Its façade features statues of explorers, including Ludwig Leichhardt and Major Thomas Mitchell. Head to **Martin Place** via George Street and check out the **GPO**'s Pitt Street colonnade with characters representing trades, professions and industries, then sneak a peek through the windows of Martin Place's grand banks. Turn right into **Macquarie Street** *(see p22)*, taking care not to bump into one of the city's "wigs", for this is Sydney's legal district. At **Hyde Park** *(see p50)*, note the lovely Art Deco **Archibald Fountain** and wander down the glorious avenue of fig trees to Park Street. Turn right and take a seat outside the classy **Bambini Trust Café** at 105 Elizabeth Street. Sample an antipasto while you peruse the Specials menu and the passers-by.

Afternoon

Head to Market Street and turn left: **Sydney Tower** is one block down on your right and the **Pitt Street Mall** *(see p00)* two blocks down. Turn into the mall and left into the **Strand Arcade** and it's time for a caffeine fix at **Luxe Espresso**. Exit at George Street and turn left. On the next corner is the **QVB** where you can spend the rest of the afternoon happily splurging.

For more city centre shopping centres and shops, see pp80–81.

Left **Food court at Skygarden** Centre **Entrance to Strand Arcade** Right **Darling Harbour**

🔟 City Shopping Centres

1 Castlereagh Street
Some of Sydney's most glamorous shopping, where you'll find international labels such as Gucci, Vuitton and Chanel. ✆ *Map M3 • Between Park St & Martin Place*

2 Pitt Street Mall
At this shopping precinct, Centrepoint, Skygarden, Mid-City Centre and Imperial Arcade offer chain stores and food outlets. Sydney Central Plaza houses the Myer department store and designer boutiques. ✆ *Map M3 • Pitt St between King & Market Sts*

3 Strand Arcade
The best of the Pitt Street arcades *(see p78)* houses gems such as Strand Hatter's, the source of authentic Akubras.

4 Queen Victoria Building
Over five levels, this heritage building houses the best of fashion, food, art, jewellery and antiques *(see p79)*. ✆ *455 George St • 9264 9209 • www.qvb.com.au*

5 Galeries Victoria
Shop for great fashion, dine in the food-court or browse at Books Kinokuniya, the largest bookshop in the southern hemisphere. ✆ *Map M4 • 500 George St • 9265 6888 • www.tgv.com.au*

MLC Centre

6 Darling Harbour
Right next to the Aquarium, Maritime and Powerhouse Museums. Stop by for a quick lunch or to buy Aussie souvenirs *(see pp28–9)*.

7 Paddy's Markets
Especially on weekends, people swarm to the fresh food section of this Chinatown hub. From clothes to souvenirs, you'll find almost anything here *(see p29)*. ✆ *Map L5 • www.paddysmarkets.com.au*

8 Market City
Situated above Paddy's Markets, this centre contains a mix of quirky Korean clothes, discount outlets and Asian food. Keep in mind that "small" is the most common size. ✆ *Map L5*

9 MLC Centre
Ideal for large budgets and corporate types. If that's you, head straight to Hunt Leather and the ready-to-wear women's designer store, Belinda *(see p100)*. ✆ *Map M3 • 19–29 Martin Place • 9224 8333 • www.mlccentre.com.au*

10 Argyle Stores
In a historic, converted warehouse, this eclectic array includes unique gift shops and fashion houses. ✆ *Map M2 • 18–24 Argyle St, The Rocks*

➡ *A trademark brand of felt hats, Akubras are distinctively Australian in their wide-brimmed style, durability and comfort.*

Interior of Dinosaur Designs

⊤10 One Of A Kind Shops

1 David Jones
Shopping at Sydney's oldest department store is a glamorous experience. DJ's stocks almost everything; pop in for a browse and a snack. ◎ *Map M4 • Elizabeth & Market Sts • 9266 5544*

2 Cancer Council of NSW
This unique shop sells everything you need to protect you from the sun including hats, clothing, beach shelters and cosmetics. Proceeds go to cancer research. ◎ *Map M4 • Shop C35, Centrepoint Westfield • 9223 9430.*

3 Done Art & Design
Loud prints of Sydney icons such as the Opera House and cockatoos adorn bright T-shirts and swimwear, hot souvenir items since the 1980s. ◎ *Map M1 • 123–25 George St • 9251 6099*

4 Mooks
Browse through Australian streetwear that's developing a following overseas. Great clothes for boys and girls, including G-Star jeans and Camper shoes. ◎ *Map M4 • Ground Floor, Galeries Victoria • 9283 8388*

5 Red Eye Records
Sydney's best range of rock music and rare records in an old-style music store. They also sell tickets to local gigs. ◎ *Map M3 • 66 King St • 9299 4233*

6 Sydney Opera House Store
This is a good place to come for souvenirs that aren't too kitsch, and some great ones that are. ◎ *Map N1 • Foyer, Sydney Opera House • 9250 7858*

7 Opals On The Rocks
Buy some of Australia's unique opals at this store in The Rocks. ◎ *Map M2 • 34–52 Harrington St • 9247 5718*

8 Dinosaur Designs
The team behind this original jewellery and homewares are some of Australia's most celebrated designers. They craft their pieces from jewel-coloured resin. ◎ *Map M3 • Strand Arcade • 9223 2953*

9 Australian Geographic Store
Australians have invented all kinds of gadgets and you'll find many of them here. Find outdoor tools and toys and great presents for children. ◎ *Map M3 • Centrepoint, Market St • 9231 5055*

10 Naturally Australian
Come here to find a bowl or box carved from one of the beautiful Australian woods such as sassafras or Huon pine. ◎ *Map M1 • 43 Circular Quay West • 9247 1531*

World-renowned Aussie wine makes an excellent souvenir or gift, and is available at all bottleshops.

Left **Live seafood tanks at Golden Century** Right **Sign for East Ocean**

Chinatown Eateries

1 Golden Century
The menu is huge, the staff are friendly and the live seafood, which includes coral trout and parrot fish, is amazing. ◈ *Map M5 • 393–399 Sussex St • 9212 3901 • www. goldencentury.com.au • No dis access • $$ • Optional BYO*

Selection of yum cha

2 The Chinese Noodle
Head to this hole-in-the-wall for homemade Chinese dumplings and noodles. ◈ *Map M6 • Thomas St Level, Prince Centre, 8 Quay St, Haymarket • 9281 9051 • No dis access • $ • Optional BYO*

3 The Regal
Away from the bustle of Dixon and Hay Streets, enjoy fine Cantonese cuisine in a classy room with impeccable decor. ◈ *Map M5 • 347–353 Sussex St • 9261 8988 • www.regal.com.au • No dis access • $$*

4 The Emperor's Garden
Their consistent and enticing menu includes classics such as Peking duck and grilled scallops. ◈ *Map M5 • 96–100 Hay St, Haymarket • 9211 2135 • $ • Optional BYO*

5 Emperor's Garden BBQ & Noodles
A meaty experience starts at the adjoining shop's window, full of hanging ducks and piglets, and ends with tasty duck and pork. ◈ *Map M6 • 213–215 Thomas St, Haymarket • 9281 9899 • $$ • Optional BYO*

6 Dragon Star Seafood
Expect great food in this room dominated by giant tanks of seafood. If you're feeling daring, try the jellyfish with pig's trotter. Yum cha daily. ◈ *Map M5 • Level 3, Market City, 9–13 Hay St, Haymarket • 9211 8988 • $$*

7 East Ocean
The food receives as much attention as the cool decor; try the braised sea cucumber or fresh abalone. ◈ *Map M5 • Haymarket East Ocean Arcade • 421–29 Sussex St • No dis access • 9212 4198 • $$*

8 Marigold
Choose from the indulgent banquet menus or stop in at lunchtime for the famous yum cha. ◈ *Map M5 • Levels 4 & 5, 683–689 George St • 9281 3388 • www.marigold.com.au • $$*

9 Passion Flower
With a fabulous range of original flavours such as lychee, taro and sticky rice, this dessert café makes a great pit stop. ◈ *Map M5 • Shop G12, Capitol Square, 730–742 George St • 9281 8322 • $*

10 Mother Chu's Vegetarian Kitchen
Warm Buddhist hospitality, canteen decor and delicious vegetarian food. Try the hot pot dishes. ◈ *Map M5 • 367 Pitt St • 9283 2828 • Closed Sun • $*

Though most of these restaurants are fully licensed, some have an optional policy of BYO, or "bring your own" alcohol.

View from Café Sydney

Price Categories

For a two course meal	**$** under $35
for one with a drink	**$$** $35–$60
(or equivalent meal),	**$$$** $60–$120
plus taxes and extra	**$$$$** $120–$200
charges.	**$$$$$** over $200

Pubs & Restaurants

1 Harbour kitchen & bar
Peace, spectacular views and exciting food make for a thoroughly enjoyable experience. ⊗ Map M1 • Park Hyatt Sydney, 7 Hickson Rd, The Rocks • 9256 1661 • $$$

2 Chinta Ria The Temple of Love
Happiness is welcomed into this lively restaurant by the giant Buddha that takes center stage. The delicious Malaysian food may be an aphrodisiac. ⊗ Map M4 • The Roof Terrace, Level 2, Cockle Bay Wharf, 201 Sussex St • 9264 3211 • $$

3 Zaaffran
This Indian restaurant offers excellent versions of all the favourites and good value set menus. ⊗ Map L4 • Level 2, 345 Harbourside Shopping Centre, Darling Harbour • 9211 8900 • $$

4 Cafe Sydney
The perfect place for a romantic dinner with its moody lighting a Mod Oz/Asian menu and gorgeous harbour views. Check out the lounge bar and jazz on Sundays. ⊗ Map N2 • Level 5, Customs House, 31 Alfred St, Circular Quay • 9251 8683 • $$$

5 Industrie–South of France
The café, bar, restaurant and club is infused with the flavour and spirit of the French Riviera, all the way from breakfast through to dinner, drinks and dancing. ⊗ Map M2 • 107 Pitt St • 9221 8001 • Open Mon–Sat • $$$

6 Slip Inn
This place has five bars over three levels including an outdoor courtyard, with Chinese Laundry nightclub on Fridays and Saturdays. ⊗ Map L3 • 111 Sussex St • 8295 9999 • Open Mon–Sat • $$

7 Cruise Bar & Restaurant
This swanky bar is perfectly placed for Opera House views and offers an extensive cocktail list. ⊗ Map M1 • Level 1–3, Overseas Passenger Terminal, West Circular Quay • 9251 1188 • $$$

8 Bar Europa
In a city of glitzy views, this underground bar makes a pleasant change. Try the delicious cocktails and bar food. ⊗ Map M3 • Basement, 82 Elizabeth St • 9232 3377 • Open Tue–Sat • $

9 Bungalow 8
It doesn't do cocktails, but punters flock to this giant waterside pub until bouncers are turning the hordes away. Get there early and be prepared for the very mainstream crowd. ⊗ Map L3 • The Promenade, King St Wharf • 9299 4000 • $$

10 Roof Bar
This rooftop hideaway offers breathtaking views of Centrepoint tower and the city skyline. Enjoy a light lunch outside on the decked terrace or sip cocktails at the bar. ⊗ Map M4 • Level 4, Skygarden Shopping Centre, 77 Castlereagh St • 9222 2122 • $

> *Unless otherwise stated, all restaurants are open daily, accept credit cards, serve vegetarian meals, and provide disabled access.*

Left **Detail of Del Rio's Façade** Right **Elizabeth Bay**

Kings Cross & Darlinghurst

THE REPUTATION OF "THE CROSS" *as a hotbed of sex and decadence may be well earned, but behind this red-light district's resident junkies and prostitutes is an interesting suburb with a rich bohemian history. Cool cafés and great Art Deco apartment buildings make up its backstreets. To the north, you'll find Potts Point with its fine Colonial villas and Victorian terrace houses, and to the east the solid middle-class enclaves of Rushcutter's Bay and Elizabeth Bay, named after Mrs Macquarie (see p20). Darlinghurst is far more hip than its northern neighbour, with a heady parade of groovers and wannabes competing with the suburb's less well-heeled residents. To the northwest is East Sydney, with its "Little Italy" centred around Stanley Street, and to the north Woolloomooloo or "the Loo", a former docklands precinct with an energetic mix of public housing estates and smart apartments.*

Left **Café on Victoria Street** Right **Neon sign marking the entrance to Kings Cross**

Sights

1. **Darlinghurst Court House & Old Darlinghurst Gaol**
2. **Sydney Jewish Museum**
3. **Victoria Street**
4. **Darlinghurst Road**
5. **El Alamein Fountain**
6. **Elizabeth Bay**
7. **The McElhone Stairs**
8. **Tusculum & Rockwall Villas**
9. **Elizabeth Bay House**
10. **Rushcutters Bay Park**

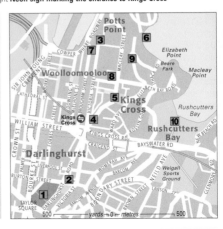

Share your travel recommendations on traveldk.com

Old Darlinghurst Gaol

3 Victoria Street

This leafy stretch of Victorian terrace houses in Potts Point was a major flashpoint during the 1970s Green Bans *(see p37)*. Pressure to demolish the terraces to make way for high-rise developments was resisted by residents and Juanita Nielsen, the local community newspaper publisher. On 4 July 1975, Nielsen attended a meeting at the Carousel Club in nearby Kings Cross; she was never seen again. Nobody in Sydney has any doubt as to the motive of her killer or killers. 🔷 *Map P3*

4 Darlinghurst Road

Darlinghurst Road runs from the court house to the Alamein Fountain. "The Wall", a sandstone wall running beside the gaol, is a nocturnal beat for male prostitutes. The pleasant Green Park is thought to be named after a former hangman at the gaol, Alexander "The Strangler" Green. Beyond the park is a colourful strip of terrace houses, hotels and cafés that ends at William Street. In the 1920s and 30s the area beyond William Street had some bohemian charm, but since WWII it has been Australia's most notorious red-light district. 🔷 *Map P4*

1 Darlinghurst Court House & Old Darlinghurst Gaol

Mortimer Lewis designed the central section of this Greek Revival court house in 1844, and James Barnet *(see p99)* designed the side wings in 1880. The 1841 Old Darlinghurst Gaol behind the court house was also designed by Mortimer Lewis and added to by James Barnet. In its early years, public hangings were conducted inside the gaol. In 1914 it became an internment facility for WWI "enemy aliens". It now houses the National Art School. 🔷 *Map P5 • Forbes St, Darlinghurst • Court House; • 9368 2947 • Open Feb–Dec: 10am–4pm Mon–Fri*

2 Sydney Jewish Museum

Following WWII almost 30,000 Holocaust survivors migrated to Australia, many of them settling in Sydney. This museum *(see p42)* explores Australian Jewish history through recordings of survivors, audio-visual displays and photographs. The ground floor deals with Jewish life following white settlement, and the upper levels focus on the Holocaust, whose survivors act as guides. 🔷 *Map P5 • 148 Darlinghurst Rd, Darlinghurst • 9360 7999 • Open 10am– 4pm Sun–Thur, 10am–2pm Fri • Adm • www.sydneyjewishmuseum.com.au*

Mr Eternity

During the Depression, a near-illiterate, reformed alcoholic took to writing "Eternity" in perfect copperplate script on pavements across the city. Arthur Stace thought he'd received instructions from God while at the Baptist Church in Darlinghurst, and he wrote the word "Eternity" half a million times before his death in 1967. An aluminium plaque in tribute to Stace can be found near the Sydney Square waterfall.

El Alamein Fountain

This dandelion-shaped fountain in the Fitzroy Gardens is especially pleasant when illuminated at night. Though many consider it overrated, it is still probably Sydney's most popularly known public artwork. Designed by Robert Woodward in 1961, it commemorates the participation of Australian soldiers in the Battle of El Alamein in Egypt during WWII, which precipitated Germany's defeat in North Africa. ❀ Map Q4 • Fitzroy Gardens: Macleay St, Elizabeth Bay • Open 24 hrs daily

El Alamein Fountain at dusk

Elizabeth Bay

A world away from the seediness of nearby Kings Cross, Elizabeth Bay's narrow, winding streets are packed with apartment buildings, including Art Deco gems such as Del Rio on Billyard Avenue, near Elizabeth Bay House. It is also home to several harbourside mansions, including Boomerang (see p15), and nearby Berthong, which Russell Crowe owned before moving up to the industrial chic of the Woolloomooloo Finger Wharf. The tiny Arthur McElhone Reserve (see p51), is overlooked by a 100 apartment balconies, but the unpretentious Beare Park can be found just down the hill, on the harbour's edge. ❀ Map Q3

The McElhone Stairs

These stone stairs link Woolloomooloo Bay with Potts Point and The Cross. Near the bottom of the stairs on Cowper Wharf Road is Harry's Café de Wheels, a pie cart that's been a Sydney late-night institution for over 50 years. Its walls are festooned with photos of famous patrons, mostly politicians and pop stars, tucking into meat pies. Nearby is the Woolloomooloo Finger Wharf (see p15), which houses upmarket bars and restaurants. ❀ Map P3

Tusculum & Rockwall Villas

"Villa conditions" were actually established in the 1830s to ensure that the hillside overlooking Woolloomooloo Bay attracted the "right sort". All new houses had to face Government House (see p21), cost a fortune, and be approved by the governor of the day. John Verge designed both Tusculum and Rockwall. The Australian Institute of Architects now occupies the former, which has a great bookshop specialising in architectural titles. Rockwall is a private residence originally built for engineer John Busby, whose bore delivered Sydney's first permanent fresh water supply. ❀ Map Q4 • Tusculum: 3 Manning St, Potts Point • Bookshop: Open 9am–5:30pm Mon–Fri, 10am–4pm Sat • Rockwall: Macleay St, Potts Point

Elizabeth Bay House

Alexander Macleay, Colonial Secretary of NSW from 1825 to 1837, had architect John Verge design this residence for his large family in 1839. Macleay was also a distinguished botanist

Tusculum Villa window

The dining room at Elizabeth Bay House

and the first president of the Australian Museum. This Greek Revival residence is said to contain the finest example of a Colonial interior anywhere in Australia. Macleay's family subdivided the original 23 ha (56 acres) of land following his death. In 1941 the house was further divided into 15 apartments. The NSW government purchased the property in the 1960s and the Historic Houses Trust undertook major restoration. It finally re-opened as a museum in 1977.
Ⓝ Map Q3 • 7 Onslow Ave, Elizabeth Bay • 9356 3022 • Open 9:30am–4pm Fri–Sun • Adm

10 Rushcutters Bay Park
Rushcutters Bay, now the mooring of choice for some of Sydney's finest yachts and the home of the Cruising Yacht Club, was the site of one of the settlers' first run-ins with the local Eora people, on 30 May 1788. The Eora speared two convicts, who were collecting rushes for roof thatching after having stolen a fishing canoe. Today, this pleasant park contains tennis courts, a quaint picket-fenced cricket ground and stadium, lovely Moreton Bay fig trees and a pleasant kiosk and café. The park is much loved by both locals and their poodles. Ⓝ Map Q4

Afternoon Meander Through Kings Cross

🕐 Begin at the El Alamein Fountain. Walk down Macleay Street and you'll pass the **Rex Hotel**, site of Sydney's first gay bar in the 1940s, the **Bottoms Up**. Turn into Greenknowe Avenue and walk down the hill and left into leafy Ithaca Road, where you'll catch glimpses of the harbour. **Beare Park** is tucked between the high-rise apartments. From the wharf there's a good view of **Boomerang**, the Spanish Mission mansion. Walk up Billyard Avenue to **Elizabeth Bay House**, passing the **Del Rio**, another Californian Spanish Mission building. Steps on Onslow Avenue will bring you back up the hill to Macleay Street.

🍽 Turning right, stroll down to **Yellow Bistro** (see p89). Have a coffee and a sweet treat on the porch.

Refreshed, walk down Challis Avenue into **Embarkation Park** for great views of the Naval Base at **Woolloomooloo**. Continue up Victoria Street, past the terrace houses in Hughes Street. Turn left into the Tusculum Street, and then Manning Street. Next door to **Tusculum Villa**, the **Werrington** and the **Wychbury** are some of the best Art Deco buildings in the Cross.

On your way back up Macleay Street, pop into Orwell Street to see the old **Metro Theatre**, where a nightclub roared in the 1930s. Finish up your afternoon tour with a drink at the **Bourbon**, a very stylishly revamped Kings Cross dive bar.

Bar at ARQ Sydney

Top 10 Gay Bars

1 ARQ Sydney
The giant dance floor here is overlooked by a mezzanine where you can people-watch. Pounding commercial house music ensures it's packed by midnight. ◎ *Map N5* • *16 Flinders St, Taylor Square* • *9380 8700* • *www.arqsydney.com.au* • *Dis access*

2 Midnight Shift Hotel
Although this stalwart of the Sydney scene is known as a meat market, it can be fun. It's usually the last stop on a club crawl. Women are not really welcome. ◎ *Map N5* • *85 Oxford St, Darlinghurst* • *9360 4319* • *www.themidnightshift.com*

3 Hellfire Club
Dark trance and techno, fetish shows and S&M gear. Discounted entry if you arrive in a fetish costume. ◎ *www.hellfiresydney.com*

4 Mars Lounge
A night for the beautiful people, in a bar popular with the fashion set thanks to its glamorous decor. Sydney icons, Alex Taylor and Chip, play vocal house music from 7pm. ◎ *Map M5* • *16 Wentworth Ave, Surry Hills* • *9267 6440* • *www. marslounge.com.au* • *Dis access*

5 Stonewall
Three levels include a bar, dance floor and lounge bar. It's patronized mostly by men and their straight girlfriends. Male Box on Wednesday nights is very popular. ◎ *Map N5* • *175 Oxford St, Darlinghurst* • *9360 1963* • *www. stonewallhotel.com*

6 Phoenix Bar
This dance bar features underground and alternative music. Dirty, held on the second Saturday of every month, is an event for men with a leather feel. ◎ *Map N5* • *Exchange Hotel basement, 34 Oxford St, Darlinghurst* • *9331 2956* • *www.exchangehotel.biz*

7 Club Kooky
An alternative to the mainstream gay clubs with a mixed crowd, good DJs, live electronic music and an anything-goes vibe. ◎ *Map N4* • *www.myspace.com/ clubkooky*

8 Flinders Hotel
The oldest gay bar in Sydney features a different event most nights. The Rock Out on the second Saturday of every month draws a mixed crowd. ◎ *Map N6* • *62 Flinders St, Darlinghurst* • *9356 3622* • *www.flindershotel.com*

9 Oxford Hotel
Its central location, Gilligan's Nightclub downstairs and two cocktail lounge bars upstairs, make the Oxford a great place to meet friends. ◎ *Map N5* • *134 Oxford St, Darlinghurst* • *9331 3467* • *www.theoxfordhotel.com.au* • *Dis access*

10 Headquarters
This is a men-only cruise club with a video lounge, a gym and regular skin and themed parties. ◎ *Map N5* • *273 Crown St, Darlinghurst* • *9331 6217* • *www. headquarters.com.au*

Male Box is a pick-up game in which men wear numbers and send "mail" (messages) to each other via a big screen.

Price Categories

For a two course meal for one with a drink (or equivalent meal), plus taxes and extra charges.

$	under $35
$$	$35–$60
$$$	$60–$120
$$$$	$120–$200
$$$$$	over $200

Interior of Lotus

Places to Eat

1 Yellow Bistro
Van-Gogh-yellow walls and creative food make one of the most famous buildings in the Cross stand out. Try the lovely brunch and the sweet selection. ◈ *Map Q3 • 57 Macleay St, Potts Point • 9357 3400 • $$*

2 Lotus
A comfortable bistro offers simple and hearty food and an effortlessly stylish crowd. ◈ *Map Q3 • 22 Challis Ave, Potts Point • 9326 9000 • Dinner Tue–Sat • $$*

3 Spring Espresso
Get coffee and snacks with Sydney's most glamorous people, where it's all about being seen. ◈ *Map Q3 • 65 Macleay St, Potts Point • 9331 0190 • No dis access • $*

4 Fratelli Paradiso
Another haunt of the style set, this time with a distinct Melbourne twist. Servings of the Italian food are small, so make sure to order some homemade pastries. ◈ *Map Q3 • 12–16 Challis Ave, Potts Point • 9357 1744 • $$*

5 Jimmy Liks
A buzzing joint with Asian-inspired cocktails that set off the fresh and delicious flavours of the curries and stir-fries. ◈ *Map P4 • 188 Victoria St, Potts Point • 8354 1400 • Dinner daily • $$*

6 Hugo's Lounge
This is just the place for a swanky night out. Great drinks and showy Mod Oz food at big-night prices. ◈ *Map P4 • Level 1, 33 Bayswater Rd, Kings Cross • 9357 4411 • Dinner Thu–Sat • $$$*

7 Buon Ricordo
Owner and chef Armando Percuoco's award-winning Italian restaurant is extremely popular with local foodies. ◈ *Map P5 • 108 Boundary St, Darlinghurst • 9360 6729 • No dis access • $$$*

8 Fu-Manchu
A tiny, excellent Chinese noodle bar with good vegetarian options. ◈ *Map P5 • 249 Victoria St, Darlinghurst • 9360 9424 • Dinner daily • No dis access • $$*

9 Ecabar
This groovy, gay and sleek corner café offers seriously good coffee and snacks. A popular meeting place to hang out and soak up the sun on their outdoor tables. ◈ *Map E4 • 128 Darlinghurst Rd, Darlinghurst • 9332 1433 • $*

10 Phamish
Fun, cheap and bustling, this Vietnamese café serves fresh and tasty food. ◈ *Map P5 • 354 Liverpool St, Darlinghurst • 9357 2688 • Dinner Tue–Sun • No dis access • $*

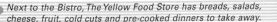

Next to the Bistro, The Yellow Food Store has breads, salads, cheese, fruit, cold cuts and pre-cooked dinners to take away.

Left **Five Ways in Paddington** Centre **Victoria Barracks** Right **Sydney Cricket Ground**

Paddington & Surry Hills

B ACK IN THE 1960S, *Paddington's neglected Victorian charms were rediscovered by "trendies" who zealously set about restoring the area's terraces. Most of Paddington's working-class residents took fright and fled to suburbs far away. Now mostly white-collar families occupy the renovated terraces, and this hilly district, bordered by Centennial Park, Moore Park, Darlinghurst and the Eastern Suburbs, is one of Sydney's smartest addresses.*

Its main strip, Oxford Street, is a window-shopper's heaven and its backstreets a delight for anyone who loves Victorian architecture. Surry Hills' charms took a little longer to be appreciated, but now this suburb rivals Darlinghurst and Newtown as one of the grooviest districts in Sydney. But it wasn't always so. During the Great Depression, Surry Hills was one of Sydney's most notorious slums and the haunt of razor gang queen Kate Leigh (see p37). This dark period in its history was perfectly captured by the writer Ruth Park (see p41).

Victorian "Iron Lace" detailing

🔟 Sights

1. Victorian Terrace Houses
2. Paddington Market
3. Paddington Town Hall
4. Juniper Hall
5. Victoria Barracks
6. Oxford & Crown Sts
7. Sydney Cricket Ground
8. Aussie Stadium
9. The Entertainment Quarter
10. Whiteley Studio

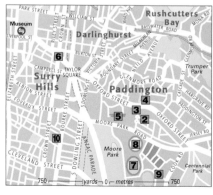

Sign up for DK's email newsletter on traveldk.com

1 Victorian Terrace Houses

Many of Paddington's lovely terrace houses, with their narrow frontages, iron-work verandas and pocket-handkerchief gardens, were erected following the construction of the Victoria Barracks *(see p92)* in the 1840s. The area went into decline during 1931's Great Depression, but an influx of migrants revitalised the area after WWII. Many of those migrants moved out following the suburb's gentrification in the 1960s and '70s. Some of the most interesting examples of the Victorian terrace style are found in Glenmore and Jersey Roads, and Cascade, Liverpool, Windsor and Paddington Streets.

2 Paddington Market

This just might be Sydney's best loved weekend market. It's held every Saturday in the shaded grounds of Paddington Village's St. John's Uniting Church. Ever since 1973, this al fresco bazaar has been a great place to shop for jewellery, crafts, fashion, pottery, soaps, second-hand clothing and the like. It's always had a New Age bent, so you're also likely to find someone who can massage those travel-weary shoulders, read your tarot cards or fine-tune your chakras. ◈ *Map Q6 • www.paddingtonmarkets.com.au*

Paddington Market

Victorian terrace houses in Paddington

3 Paddington Town Hall

This Classical Revival Town Hall on Oxford Street was designed by J Kemp, a local architect who won an international competition to design a civic centre that matched the suburb's increasing status. The main building was completed in 1891, and the clock tower that now dominates was added several years later. The hall underwent extensive restoration work in the 1990s and is no longer used by the council. But it does house the suburb's library, offices, and a radio station. It is also a regular venue for private functions and corporate events. ◈ *Map Q6*

4 Juniper Hall

Robert Cooper (1776–1857) was one of Sydney's more successful emancipists and a self-confessed smuggler. Originally sent down for receiving stolen goods, Cooper made a small fortune as Sydney's first distiller, specialising in gin flavoured with juniper berries: hence the name of this residence. Situated diagonally opposite the Town Hall, Juniper Hall was built in 1824 to house his 20 children from three marriages. The house was threatened with demolition for several years, but finally spared in the 1980s and restored by the National Trust. ◈ *Map Q6*

Around Town – Paddington & Surry Hills

5 Victoria Barracks

Occupying 12 ha (30 acres), these barracks were built between 1841 and 1848. They are immediately recognisable from Oxford Street by their high sandstone walls; many regard this complex of late Georgian buildings as one of the finest military barracks in the world. The architect was Major George Barney, who also designed Fort Denison (see p38). Until 1870 the barracks were home to British troops; today they are an Australian Army facility. The Army Museum is housed in the former military prison and contains several interesting exhibits tracing the military heritage of New South Wales. ® *Map P6* • *Oxford St* • *Open 10am–1pm Thu, 10am–3pm Sun; tours 10am Thu* • *Army Museum: 9339 3330* • *Open 10am–12:30pm Thur, 10am–4pm Sun*

6 Oxford & Crown Streets

Despite recent upheavals, Oxford Street is reclaiming its reputation as Sydney's most fashion-conscious shopping strip with distinctive boutiques. Although it runs all the way from Hyde Park to Bondi Junction, the prime shopping drag is on the north side of the road between Barcom Avenue and Queen Street (see p97), which runs down to Woollahra. Surry Hills' Crown Street is less conspicuous and polished than its northern rival, but it's gaining a reputation as a good spot to source homewares, designer and retro furniture and fashion items. It has some great cafés, ethnic restaurants and grocers, pubs and factory outlets. ® *Map N5*

Sydney Cricket Ground

7 Sydney Cricket Ground

Stationed at Victoria Barracks in 1851, the British Army were told to take their bats and balls and entertain themselves on the empty land south of the barracks. Ever since, this site (see p53) has been the spiritual home for millions of cricket-mad Sydneysiders. In January 1928, fans saw Sir Donald Bradman's first-class cricket debut and, in January 2004, Australian Test Captain, Steve Waugh, took his final bow here. It has also hosted concerts by the Rolling Stones, Madonna and Green Day, as well as Australian Rules Football matches.

8 Aussie Stadium

Designed by Phillip Cox, this stadium (see pp47 & 53) was completed in 1988 to coincide with Australia's Bicentenary. The ground was ostensibly designed for Sydney's preferred football code, Rugby League, but it has occasionally permitted upstarts from the southern code, Australian Rules, to take to the field. Soccer was played here during the 2000 Sydney Olympics and has now become a regular event. The Stadium has also held several concert performances, which have included

Entrance to Victoria Barracks

shows by U2, Robbie Williams and Barbra Streisand.
🕐 *Sportspace Tours of Aussie Stadium, SCG and Cricket Museum: 1300 724 737 • 10am, noon & 2pm Mon–Fri, 10am Sat • Adm*

9 The Entertainment Quarter
This massive entertainment complex houses a variety of restaurants including award-winning Chinese, traditional Italian, the Bavarian Bier Café and modern Australian dining. Entertainment options include two movie complexes, bowling, pool, karaoke, a Comedy Store and three pubs. Late night shopping is open every night in an open-air area. There are two kids' playgrounds and two child entertainment venues. The EQ is also home to two of the best markets in Sydney, The EQ Farmers' Market and Sydney's Bent Street Bazaar merchandise market. 🕐 *Map E6 • Lang Rd, Moore Park • Farmers' Market: 10am–3:30pm Wed & Sat • Bent Street Bazaar Market: 10am–4pm Sun • Most shops open 10am–10pm daily • www.eqmoorepark.com.au*

10 Whiteley Studio
Tucked down a Surry Hills backstreet, the former studio of artist Brett Whiteley *(see pp26 & 44)* is now a public museum and art gallery. Whiteley painted some of Sydney's most iconic works. He loved the harbour and the nude, and both feature in his paintings. In 1985 he converted this former factory into a studio hut, just seven years later, he was found dead from a heroin overdose in a motel room in the south coast township of Thirroul. The gallery has regular exhibitions and displays the artist's studio much as it was before he died.

A Morning Stroll Through Paddington

🕐 From the **Darlinghurst Court House** *(see p85)* follow Oxford Street as far as the imposing sandstone walls of **Victoria Barracks**. Turn left into Glenmore Road, which has a cluster of small but classy boutiques. Gipps Street leads to Liverpool Street, which is a winding road of elegant double-storey terraces reminiscent of some of London's wealthier Victorian districts. **Hogarth Galleries** *(see p45)*, is down Walker Lane. Rejoin Glenmore Road and follow this winding and busy thoroughfare to **Five Ways**, a quaint little intersection with several good cafés, including **Gusto**.

After coffee and a snack, head up Broughton Street to the narrow laneway and steps on your left. At the bottom of the lane turn right and walk down to steep Cascade Street. Turn right and walk uphill past Windsor Street's incredibly narrow terraces to Paddington Street. Follow this elegant fig tree-lined avenue up to Jersey Road, passing **Tim Olsen Gallery** *(see p45)* and several of Sydney's premier addresses en route. Turn right into Jersey Road, then into narrow Caledonia Street, which leads back to McGarvie Street where several eccentric balconies overhang the narrow pavement. Turn into Underwood Street and you'll find the **London Tavern**, happy to serve you a well-earned drink. The pub has a superb bistro attached and is located near William Street, which also has several boutiques.

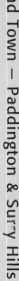

Around Town – Paddington & Surry Hills

93

Left **Display at Mecca Cosmetica** Right **Interior of Zimmermann**

TOP 10 Fashion & Homewares

1 Orson & Blake
This one-stop shop for the hippest of hip combines a boutique, bookshop, furniture showroom, café and gallery. ✪ *Map D5 • 483 Riley St, Surry Hills • 8399 2525 • www.orsonandblake.com.au*

2 Planet
There's plenty that's portable here, such as wonderful textiles and ceramics. Each piece comes with information about its creator, and can be giftwrapped. ✪ *Map N6 • 419 Crown St, Surry Hills • 9698 0680 • www.planetfurniture.com.au*

3 Capital L
All the hottest names in Aussie design are crammed into this tiny shop. ✪ *Map P6 • 333 South Dowling St, Darlinghurst • 9361 0111 • www.capital-l.com.*

4 Mecca Cosmetica
Mecca stocks cult cosmetic brands such as Kiehl's and Stila, and is happy to advise on their application. ✪ *Map P6 • 126 Oxford St, Paddington • 9361 4488 • www.meccacosmetica.com.au*

5 Von Troska
This long-established Paddington designer started with five dresses and a stall at Paddington Markets in 1984. Timeless designs created using rich textures and material.
✪ *Map Q6 • 294 Oxford St, Paddington • 9360 7522 • www.vontroska.com.au*

6 Andrew McDonald
On a street of designer names, this little shop may not stand out. But it hand-crafts gor-geous shoes for men and women. ✪ *Map Q6 • 58 William St, Paddington • 9358 6793 • www.andrewmcdonald.com.au*

7 Zimmermann
Check out the fantastic range of women's swimwear and gorgeous clothing collection. ✪ *Map P6 • 387 Oxford St, Paddington • 9357 4700 • www.zimmermannwear.com*

8 Easton Pearson
This much-lauded designer duo specialises in unusual textiles and embellishments. Favoured by a slightly older clientele who can afford the hefty price tags. ✪ *Map R6 • 18 Elizabeth St, Paddington • 9331 4433*

9 Cloth
Bold, original designs are hand-screened onto natural fibres. Buy lengths of fabric or soft furnishings such as cushions. ✪ *Map D5 • 35 Buckingham St, Surry Hills • 9699 2266 • www.clothfabric.com*

10 Akira
Nothing compares to Akira's one-of-a-kind designs; his delicate and ephemeral garments are virtually art pieces and coveted by all. ✪ *Map F5 • 12A Queen St, Woollahra • 9361 5221 • www.akira.com.au*

Cushions at Cloth

➜ *If you need a break during shopping, stop for a bite at Sloane, 312 Oxford Street.*

Price Categories

For a two course meal for one with a drink (or equivalent meal), plus taxes and extra charges.

$	under $35
$$	$35–$60
$$$	$60–$120
$$$$	$120–$200
$$$$$	over $200

The entrance to Red Lantern

TOP 10 Hot Spots

1 Red Lantern
A relaxed atmosphere and red interior add to the fun, but also go for the fresh and spicy southern Vietnamese food and good vegetarian options. Booking is essential. ◎ *Map D5 • 545 Crown St, Surry Hills • 9698 4355 • Tue–Sun dinner, Tue–Fri lunch • $$*

2 Il Baretto
It's always packed and you can't reserve, but they'll send you to a nearby pub and collect you when a table's ready. Cheap, authentic and delicious pasta. ◎ *Map D5 • 496 Bourke St, Surry Hills • 9361 6163 • Open Mon–Sat • BYO • No credit cards • $*

3 Mahjong Room
Shanghai-style Chinese food, served on carved wooden mahjong tables, offers that important comfort factor. ◎ *Map N5 • 312 Crown St, Darlinghurst • 9361 3985 • Mon–Sat dinner • BYO • $$*

4 Uchi Lounge
The warm but minimal design of this small bar provides excellent environs for the fusion French-Japanese food. ◎ *Map N5 • 15 Brisbane St, Darlinghurst • 9261 3524 • Mon–Sat dinner, Thu–Fri lunch • $*

5 Assiette
Local foodies lamenting the loss of Bécause were delighted when Assiette arrived with its fine modern European cuisine. ◎ *Map D3 • 48 Albion St, Surry Hills • 9212 7979 • Tue–Sat dinner, Fri lunch • $$–$$$*

6 Hotel Hollywood
This grungy dive bar is the perfect antidote to the super-glam Sydney experience. Meet groovy art students, designers and musicians. ◎ *Map M5 • 2 Foster St, Surry Hills • 9281 2765*

7 Clock Hotel
This place surges into life after work with locals revelling in happy hour throughout its four bars. ◎ *Map D5 • 470 Crown St, Surry Hills • 9331 5333 • $$*

8 Light Brigade Hotel
Bypass the spruced-up sports bar and head upstairs to a fantastic bistro-pub for a feast. ◎ *Map E5 • 2a Oxford St, Woollahra • 9331 2930 • $*

9 Middle Bar
Sip a cocktail and watch Taylor Square from the balcony of this bar, which maintains the perfect balance of glitz and hip. ◎ *Map N5 • Kinselas, 383 Bourke St, Taylor Square, Darlinghurst • 9331 3100*

10 Goodbar
One of Sydney's most popular and longest-established nightclubs. ◎ *Map P6 • 11a Oxford St, Paddington • 9360 6759*

Unless otherwise stated, all restaurants are open daily, accept credit cards, serve vegetarian meals and provide disabled access.

95

Left **Detail on the Macquarie Lighthouse** Right **Beachside at Watsons Bay**

Eastern Suburbs

I F YOU'VE GOT THE MONEY *this is a fantastic place to buy real estate, especially on the harbour. In Colonial times, some of Sydney's wealthiest citizens built country estates on these north-facing slopes overlooking the water. These were later subdivided, but the Eastern Suburbs remain leafy, manicured and ever-so-well spoken. With exclusive private schools, million-dollar marinas, golf clubs and more salons and day spas than you can count, the Eastern Suburbs are absolutely "gorgeous". There are several idyllic harbourside beaches and swimming pools, and numerous harbourside and parkland walking options. If you're lucky, you might even spot the rare and endangered "blue-rinse", a hairstyle once favoured by Eastern Suburbs dowagers that could almost qualify as a heritage-listed feature. If spending*

money is your thing, rest assured: where there's money, there's shopping. And the Eastern Suburbs have some prime retail strips, especially in Woollahra and Double Bay.

The Gap

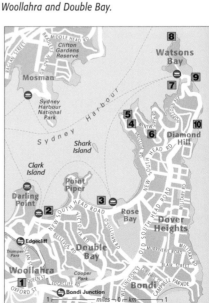

Sights

1. Queen Street
2. Double Bay
3. Rose Bay
4. Nielsen Park
5. Greycliffe House
6. Vaucluse House
7. Watsons Bay
8. Camp Cove & South Head
9. The Gap
10. Macquarie Lighthouse

Share your travel recommendations on traveldk.com

Queen Street

Queen Street
You won't find any rustic treasures in the antiques shops that line this leafy street downhill from Paddington's Oxford Street. Items here are super expensive, such as Louis XIV clocks, original Colonial prints, 18th-century Persian rugs, and estate jewellery. Even if your wallet is drained, it's still a fun place to window-shop and there are some excellent cafés nearby. ✪ *Map F5*

Double Bay
The immense wealth of "Double Pay" is almost a joke; people call it the plastic surgery capital of Australia. To the west is exclusive Darling Point, where you'll find Major Mitchell's *(see p9)* former harbourside residence on Carthona Avenue. To the east is Point Piper, which was home to Sir Lawrence Hargrave *(see p31)* from 1902 to 1915. In between is Steyne Park and the delightful Redleaf Pool, just below the lovely Blackburn Gardens on New South Head Road. William Street, Bay Street and New South Head Road border the main shopping precinct, where you'll find all the best international retail stores. ✪ *Map F4*

Rose Bay
The largest cove in Sydney Harbour is embraced by Point Piper to the west and Vaucluse to the east. Northeast of Point Piper is Shark Island *(see p15)*. To the east is Hermit Point, reputedly the haunt of a reclusive former convict. In 1942 a Japanese submarine lobbed shells into Rose Bay, presumably aiming for the former flying-boat base; it's still the base for Sydney Harbour's seaplanes *(see p17)*. If you've followed New South Head Road over from Double Bay, you'll enjoy the walk along the waterfront from Rose Bay Park to Lyne Park. ✪ *Map G4*

Nielsen Park
Part of Sydney Harbour National Park, Nielsen Park *(see p51)* makes its way from winding Vaucluse Road down to Shark Bay, so named for the sharks caught here in the days before shark nets. In the centre of the park is the Mt Trefle Walk, and near the beach are changing pavilions, a great kiosk, Greycliffe House *(see p98)* and a memorial to the Harbour Foreshore Vigilance Committee *(see p15)*. The Hermitage Foreshore Walk starts west of Shark Beach, and offers some of the best views of Sydney as it meanders along the shoreline back to Rose Bay via Hermit Point. Don't forget your swimsuit.

Snakes Alive
The lush grounds of Vaucluse House *(see p98)* owe a debt of gratitude to Sir Henry Browne Hayes. This Irish baronet, exiled for kidnapping a Quaker heiress, was so petrified of snakes that he imported tons of turf blessed by St Patrick in an effort to rid his 205-ha (508-acre) estate of the scaly vermin.

Left **Greycliffe House in Nielsen Park** Right **Watsons Bay**

Greycliffe House

After WC Wentworth's *(see p37 & below)* daughter was married, her husband commissioned the architect John Hilly to construct this Gothic residence. However, the couple left for England before its 1851 completion. It later became a home for mothers and babies, before the NSW government purchased the property in 1911. The ground floor is now open to the public, while the NPWS *(see p14)* occupies the rest of the building. ⚐ *Map G2 • Nielsen Park • 9337 5511*

Vaucluse House

William Charles Wentworth purchased this property which was built in 1803, in 1827. Wentworth was a major figure in the early colony – a barrister, explorer and statesman, he railed against the privileges enjoyed by the English-born colonists and lobbied for self-government. The Wentworths lived in this Gothic house until 1861. It has been a public museum since 1910. ⚐ *Map H2 • Wentworth Rd, Vaucluse • 9388 7922 • Open 9:30am–4pm Fri–Sun • Adm*

Watsons Bay

Named after Robert Watson, the quartermaster on the HMS *Sirius (see p79)*, this bay has been the base for Sydney Harbour's pilot boats since the 1800s. Uphill from Robertson Park are the Greycliffe Memorial Gates, which commemorate the 41 people who lost their lives when the ferry *Greycliffe* went down in 1927. ⚐ *Map H1*

Camp Cove & South Head

Just north of Watsons Bay is Camp Cove, where Governor Phillip spent the night after decamping from Botany Bay *(see pp36 & 38)* and entered Port Jackson for the first time. A track leads from the kiosk at the northern end of this protected beach over to tiny male-nudist Lady Bay Beach, which is overlooked by the HMAS *Watson* Naval Base. At the end of the track is South Head's Hornby Lighthouse and several old gun emplacements *(see p51)*. This windswept headland offers spectacular views out to sea, across to Manly and the North Harbour. ⚐ *Map H1*

Vaucluse House

The Gap

9 Perhaps Sydney's most infamous headland, this bluff, overlooking the ocean and the wave-lashed rocks far below, has seen more than its fair share of suicides. South of The Gap is the rusting anchor of the *Dunbar* *(see p36)* and further south again is Jacob's Ladder: the sole survivor of the 1857 *Dunbar* tragedy was hauled to safety up this cleft in the rocks. Further south again is the signal station that has been monitoring shipping in and out of Sydney Harbour since 1848. ◈ *Map H1*

Macquarie Lighthouse

Macquarie Lighthouse

10 Australia's longest continuously operating lighthouse stands on the windswept clifftops of Vaucluse. The original lighthouse, built between 1816 and 1818, was designed by noted convict architect Francis Greenway *(see p23)*. It was the first of many projects Greenway completed for Governor Macquarie, earning him a conditional pardon. Within 60 years of its construction the eroded tower was held together with iron bands and in 1883 a new lighthouse was built by architect James Barnet *(see p85)* to closely resemble the original. The tower is open to the public every two months. ◈ *Map H2* • *www.harbourtrust.gov.au*

An Eastern Suburbs Stroll

Morning

🕐 Catch the Bondi Explorer or a 325 bus from **Circular Quay** *(see p18)* and get off at **Nielsen Park**. It's a short walk downhill to **Greycliffe House** and **Shark Beach**. When you're ready, walk back to Vaucluse Road, which becomes Wentworth Road. The entrance to **Vaucluse House** is further down on the right. Continue along Wentworth and take the first right into Chapel Road. WC Wentworth's gloomy mausoleum is just up the hill on your left. Steps lead from behind the mausoleum to Fitzwilliam Street. Turn right and walk downhill to the lane on your left, which takes you across the Parsley Bay suspension footbridge. Take the steps on your left leading up to **The Crescent** and follow this around until you reach Palmerston Street, which leads to **Watsons Bay Pilot Station**. Follow Marine Parade north to the ferry wharf and lunch at **Doyle's** *(see p101)*.

Afternoon

After lunch, walk to Short Street at the end of the beach, turn immediately left into Cove Street, and then left again into Pacific Street. This leads up to **Green Point** overlooking **Camp Cove**. After enjoying a swim here, or at **Lady Bay Beach** further on, follow the path along the clifftops to **South Head**. Retrace your steps and catch the ferry from **Watsons Bay** back to Circular Quay, or the bus from Hopetoun Avenue.

Around Town – Eastern Suburbs

Left **Jan Logan's interior** Centre **Jewellery at Jan Logan** Right **Incense at Angsana Spa**

🔟 Luxury Shopping

1 Axel Mano
If you're planning some time in the sun, come here to find that very special hat. ⬡ *Map F5 • 46a Ocean St, Woollahra • 9362 3756*

2 Jan Logan
Logan is considered the doyenne of Australian jewellery, offering exquisite creations crafted from precious and semi-precious stones. ⬡ *Map F4 • 36 Cross St, Double Bay • 9363 2529*

3 Joh Bailey
Get a haircut, style and expert colour from Sydney's hairdresser to the stars. ⬡ *Map F4 • 7 Knox St, Double Bay • 9363 4111*

4 Angsana Spa
Angsana's Thailand-trained therapists offer 39 relaxing holistic treatments. ⬡ *Map F4 • 15 Bay St, Double Bay • 9328 5501*

5 Bulb
Find leisurewear designed for lounging, sleeping and yoga, as well as beauty products and fragrances. ⬡ *Map F4 • 10 Transvaal Ave, Double Bay • 9328 5900*

6 Belinda
This women's designer store stocks gorgeous labels such as Marni. A Belinda shoe emporium is around the corner. ⬡ *Map F4 • 8 Transvaal Ave, Double Bay • 9328 6288*

7 Sheil Abbey
Though not as glamorous as some of its neighbours, this shop offers unique Australian gifts. Look out for handmade platters and bowls engraved with gum leaves. ⬡ *Map F4 • Cooper & Bay Sts, Double Bay • 9363 9121*

8 Lesley McKay's Bookshop
A great bookshop with helpful and knowledgable staff, and couches for settling in with your finds. ⬡ *Map F4 • 118 Queen St, Woollahara • 9328 2733*

9 WBJ
This shopping centre brings the concept of luxury malls to Sydney, with dozens of designer boutiques such as Morrissey, Marcs and Leona Edmiston. ⬡ *Map F5 • 500 Oxford St, Bondi Junction • 9947 8000*

10 Collette Dinnigan
This multi award winning designer creates beautifully crafted women's clothing. Fans of her prized designs include Nicole Kidman, Cate Blanchett and Jerry Hall. ⬡ *Map Q6 • 33 William St, Paddington • 9360 6691*

There are several branches of Belinda scattered around Sydney; for the store at the MLC Centre see p80.

Doyle's On The Beach

Price Categories

For a two course meal for one with a drink (or equivalent meal), plus taxes and extra charges.

$	under $35
$$	$35–$60
$$$	$60–$120
$$$$	$120–$200
$$$$$	over $200

⑩ Relaxed Dining

1 Nina's Ploy Thai
A popular year-round eatery serving traditional Thai cuisine. In summer, the outdoor tables fill quickly with Bondi locals. ◈ *Map H5 • 132d, E Waisoa Ave, Bondi • 9365 1118 • $*

2 Bukhara
Indian cuisine with a Mauritian touch and friendly service distinguishes this neighbourhood restaurant. ◈ *Map F4 • 55 Bay St, Double Bay • 9363 5510 • No dis access • $$–$$$*

3 Vamps Bistro
Traditional French cuisine in the heart of Paddington means this long-established restaurant is full of locals every night. ◈ *Map E4 • 227 Glenmore Rd, Paddington • 9931 1032 • Tue–Sat dinner, Sat, Sun lunch • $$*

4 Pompei
Pompei is renowned for its authentic thin-crust pizza and myriad gelato flavours.
◈ *Map G5 • 126 Roscoe St, Bondi Beach • 9365 1233 • $$*

A packed day at Barzura

5 Seasalt
Smart food and a great location make this beachside café very appealing. ◈ *Map U4 • 1 Donnellan Circuit, Clovelly • 9664 5344 • $$*

6 Barzura
At this large eatery, relaxed all-day meals, outdoor tables and beach views make for a great time. ◈ *Map U5 • 62 Carr St, Coogee • 9665 5546 • No dis access • $$*

7 Restaurant Balzac
Excellent food, reasonable prices and great service make this local bistro a relaxing stop. ◈ *Map U4 • 141 Belmore Rd, Randwick • 9399 9660 • Bookings essential • Dinner Tue–Sat, lunch Fri • $$$*

8 Blue Orange
This casual café changes into an intimate restaurant, with a mix of European, Asian and African cuisine. ◈ *Map H5 • 49 Hall St, Bondi Beach • 9300 9885 • $$$*

9 Catalina
Contemporary Australian cuisine with Italian and Spanish influences. The interior is elegant and the views superb. ◈ *Map G4 • 1 Sutherland Ave, Rose Bay • 9371 0555 • Mon–Sat dinner, lunch daily • $$$*

10 Doyle's On The Beach
A stalwart of the Sydney scene that has seen better days, but still draws in the crowds for fish and chips on the beach. ◈ *Map H2 • 11 Marine Parade, Watsons Bay • 9337 2007 • No dis access • $$$*

Unless otherwise stated, all restaurants are open daily, accept credit cards, serve vegetarian meals and provide disabled access.

Left **King Street** Centre **Crabs at the Sydney Fish Market** Right **Entrance of Gleebooks**

Newtown & Glebe

A FEW YEARS AGO, *Newtown didn't even register a blip on the tourist radar. But a trendy crowd has recently given this suburb the raffish charm that several other suburbs have lost since falling victim to Sydney's relentless inner-city gentrification. It's still a bit rough around the edges, which makes it a great place to shop for funky clothes, books and retro furnishings, and it has some groovy cafés. Glebe, on the other hand, is almost the grand dame of gentrified inner-city suburbs. In 1789, Governor Phillip granted the chaplain of the First Fleet, Reverend Richard Johnson, 162 ha (400 acres) for services rendered. Today, Glebe accommodates workers' cottages and impressive 19th-century residences on tree-lined streets that meander down to the harbour. It is also home to numerous cafés and restaurants, an arthouse cinema, Sydney's best bookshop Gleebooks, pleasant harbourside parks and the ever-popular Glebe Market.*

Waterfront cafés at the Sydney Fish Market

🔟 Sights

1. Sydney Park
2. King Street
3. Camperdown Cemetery
4. Sydney University
5. Glebe Point Road
6. Glebe Market
7. Sze Yup Buddhist Chinese Temple
8. Jubilee, Bicentennial & Federal Parks
9. Anzac Bridge
10. Sydney Fish Market

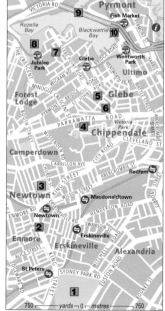

1 Sydney Park

The entrance to Sydney Park is marked by four giant chimneys once used for the huge kilns of the Sydney brickworks. Clever park landscaping incorporated parts of the brick works, so that you walk over a courtyard paved with hand-moulded bricks. The grassy slopes of the park make it a favourite with local dog-walkers and offer a wonderful view of the city from the hills. It is a welcome wide open space, rare in Sydney. ® *Map C6*
• *Sydney Park Rd & King St, St Peters*

2 King Street

Originally known as Cooks River Road, King Street has been an important thoroughfare since the days of European settlement, when it linked Sydney Town with farms in the Cooks River Basin. Newtown once belonged to a few rich men, but by the late 1800s it had become a thriving township. By then King Street looked much as it does today, bustling and lined with shops. Many stately homes on the streets off King Street have been restored, but most of the houses began as poor workers' cottages. Migrants arrived in the 1960s and '70s, along with rockers, goths and punks, and Newtown is still peopled by an eclectic mix. Above the grungy street level, you'll see that the upper façades of many shopfronts have retained Victorian plasterwork detail. ® *Map C5*

3 Camperdown Cemetery

Sydney's oldest remaining cemetery lies in the grounds of St Stephen's Church. When the cemetery was established in 1848, it was one of three serving all of Sydney. Many historic figures are buried here, including Alexander Macleay *(see p86)*, Colonial Secretary from 1826 to 1837. When the *Dunbar* sank just outside Sydney Heads in 1857 *(see p36)*, the bodies recovered were buried in a mass grave at Camperdown and a memorial was erected for them. Eliza Donnithorne, thought to be the inspiration for Charles Dickens' Miss Havisham, also lies there. While walking the peaceful paths, note the gravestones lining the walls. These original stones were moved inside when the outer area was turned into a park. ® *Map B5* • *Church St, Newtown* • *Open daylight hours*

4 Sydney University

Australia's first university was founded in 1850. Many of the buildings on the large campus are of little architectural merit, but the Main Quadrangle building makes the university well worth a visit. Designed to mimic the hallowed halls of Oxford and Cambridge, its ornate Victorian Gothic façade is adorned with gargoyles and pinnacles. The Nicholson Museum of antiquities is housed in one wing, and the Macleay Museum is also close by *(see p43)*. ® *Map C5*

Main Quadrangle at Sydney University

Sze Yup Buddhist Chinese Temple

5 Glebe Point Road

Glebe came about as a series of land grants to wealthy free settlers. Two remaining Regency villas, Toxteth Park and Lyndhurst, were designed by celebrated Colonial architect John Verge. Today it is a hippie enclave characterised by New Age and health food shops and laidback locals. Leafy and settled into hills with harbour views, the area has a village atmosphere. Glebe Point Road runs through the centre, from Broadway up to the water at Jubilee Point, and is lined with shops and cafés. To experience Glebe's bohemian side, pop into Sappho bookshop and café for a latte then head to the Excelsior pub for some eclectic live gigs. ◈ Map J5 • Toxteth Park: St Scholasticas College, Arcadia St • Lyndhurst: 61 Darghan St • Excelsior: 101 Bridge Rd • 9660 7479 • Sappho: 51 Glebe Point Rd • 9552 4498

6 Glebe Market

Every Saturday from 10am–4pm, the grounds of Glebe Public School are used by market stalls selling new and second-hand clothes, records and bric-a-brac. A great source for flares, leather jackets and sunglasses, Glebe Market offers great bargains. ◈ Map K6

Wares at Glebe Market

7 Sze Yup Buddhist Chinese Temple

Sydney saw its first influx of Chinese immigrants soon after the discovery of gold in the 1850s. The city's Chinese community, the largest in Australia, built this temple on the site of a former market garden in 1898. It is named after a district in the Chinese province of Kwongtung. The traditional red and green temple was restored in 1978 and the archway added in 1982. The bones of the deceased were once kept here before their return to China for burial. Visitors are welcome, but do remember that this is an active place of worship and not a tourist attraction. ◈ Map B4 • Edward St • Open 9am–5pm daily

Incense burning at the temple

8 Jubilee, Bicentennial & Federal Parks

These three contiguous parks overlooking Rozelle Bay offer fantastic views of the city and the working harbour. A pathway follows the north shoreline overlooking the container terminal on the other side of Rozelle Bay. To the west, just over the footbridge, is a great children's playground. And to the south is the old railway viaduct which threads its way past the historic grandstand in Jubilee Park. The small Pope Paul VI Reserve has one of the best views in Sydney, looking across Blackwattle Bay to the Anzac and Sydney Harbour Bridges. ◈ Map B4

9 Anzac Bridge

This stunning bridge was named in honour of Australia's WWI soldiers: Anzac stands for Australian and New Zealand Army Corps. It spans narrow Johnstons Bay and links Pyrmont with Rozelle and Balmain *(see p108)*. Opened in 1995, this is the longest cable-stayed span bridge in Australia, and many consider it Sydney's finest. A pedestrian path runs beside the inbound lanes and is accessible from Quarry Master Drive, north of the Sydney Fish Market. It offers great views of the city in the distance and the adjacent swing-span 1901 Glebe Island Bridge below. ◈ Map J3

Anzac Bridge

10 Sydney Fish Market

The largest market of its kind in the Southern Hemisphere, this complex in Pyrmont is home to the fishing fleet, wholesale and retail fish markets, delicatessens, oyster bars, sushi and sashimi bars, cafés, restaurants, and even a bakery. You can enjoy some of the most exquisitely cooked seafood, or just slum it with equally delectable fish and chips. The Fish Market contains the Sydney Seafood School, where some of Australia's biggest-name chefs run classes such as filetting and specialist ethnic cuisines. ◈ Map K4 • Sydney Fish Market, Bank St, Pyrmont • Opens daily at 7am • 9004 1100 • Sydney Seafood School: 9004 1111 • www. sydneyfishmarket.com.au

Downhill From Newtown to Glebe

Morning

Start your day in classic Newtown style with a strong coffee at **Barmuda**, 283 Australia Street. Then follow Australia Street to Lennox Street and turn right. At the end is **St Stephen's Church**, designed by Edmund Blacket *(see p79)*. Beside the church is the entrance to the historic, peaceful **Camperdown Cemetery**. Soak up the Gothic atmosphere before heading back to hectic King Street. Check out the bookshops, cafés and funky clothing stores that run almost as far as Little Queen Street. Turn left, cross over Carillon Avenue and enter the manicured grounds of the **Sydney University**. Turn right into Physics Lane, left into Fisher Road, and right into Manning Road, reaching the archway that leads through to the Main Quadrangle. Pass beneath the Gothic Revival clock tower and wander down University Avenue to the open space of **Victoria Park**. Finally, head to bohemian Glebe Point Road to **Badde Manors** *(see p107)* for lunch.

Afternoon

Follow Glebe Point Road to Pendrill Street, turn left and follow the scent of incense downhill to the **Sze Yup Temple**. Turn right into Edward Street, left into Eglington Lane, and right again into Edward Lane to reach **Jubilee Park**. The **Pope Paul VI Reserve** can be found in the northeast corner. When done, catch a 431 or 434 bus back to town.

Left **Gleebooks** Right **C's Flash Back**

TOP 10 Funky Shops

1 Crumpler
Need a bag that will last your lifetime? That's the guarantee Crumpler gives you on their backpacks, laptop carriers, iPod holders and bean bags. ◎ *Map B5 • 305 King St • Newtown • 9565 1611*

2 Peel
Mostly devoted to the label Peel, this store also offers several other great Aussie and imported labels. ◎ *Map C5 • 120 King St, Newtown • 9557 9400*

3 Dragstar
Newtown girls love a bit of retro styling, and this is where they find it. New clothes in the style of traditional favourites include T-shirt dresses, minis, shorts and tanks. ◎ *Map B6 • 535a King St, Newtown • 9550 1243*

4 Gleebooks
This famous store is crammed with books, including academic and obscure titles, and holds weekly events such as book launches and poetry readings. ◎ *Map K6 • 49 Glebe Point Rd, Glebe • 9660 2333*

5 C's Flash Back
King Street has a few second-hand clothes shops and this is the best of them, carefully divided for easy browsing. ◎ *Map C5 • 180 King St, Newtown • 9565 4343*

6 Platypus Shoes
If the name doesn't get you, the range of shoes will. Find anything from Aussie Blundstone workboots to the most trendy trainers. ◎ *Map B5 • 275 King St, Newtown • 9557 4599*

7 Yoshi Jones
Simple garments feature Japanese silks, kimono fabrics or Oriental-inspired designs. You can also find obis and quirky accessories. ◎ *Map C5 • 134 King St, Newtown • 9550 1663*

8 Faster Pussycat
In this shrine to all things rock and rockabilly, find punk T-shirts, 1950s skirts, studded belts, magazines, music and much more. ◎ *Map B6 • 431a King St, Newtown • 9519 1744*

9 Florilegium
Most Australians have gardens, and this bookshop specialises in titles to inspire and advise on tending them all.
◎ *Map J6 • 145 St. Johns Rd, Glebe • 9571 8222*

10 Industrie
Not so original but highly affordable men's clothes range from smart to casual. Part of a chain, this is the place to go if you want a lookalike of the latest Diesel. ◎ *Map C5 • 239 King St, Newtown • 9519 7577*

Gleebooks' children's and second-hand bookshop is a few blocks up the road at 191 Glebe Point Road, Glebe; 9552 2526.

Badde Manors Café

Price Categories

For a two course meal for one with a drink (or equivalent meal), plus taxes and extra charges.	$ under $35
	$$ $35–$60
	$$$ $60–$120
	$$$$ $120–$200
	$$$$$ over $200

⁜10 Cheap Eats

1 Twelve
Enjoy food with a northern Italian influence in this buzzing restaurant with an open kitchen. ◈ Map C5 • 218 King St, Newtown • 9519 9412 • Dinner Tue–Sat • $$

2 Linda's on King St
For many years, Linda's was a well-kept local secret hidden at the back of a hotel. Today, it has been discovered and its modern Australian food is so popular that bookings are essential. ◈ Map B5 • 341 King St, Newtown • 9550 6015 • Dinner Tue–Sat • $$

3 Sumalee Thai
This one tops Newtown's many great Thai restaurants because it's in an outdoor court-yard. Enjoy the sultry flavours on a balmy summer evening ◈ Map B6 • Bank Hotel, 324 King St, Newtown • 8568 1988 • No dis access • $

4 Wedgetail
The wood-fire oven pumps out tasty thin crust pizzas with toppings such as salami, baby octopus, roasted eggplant, caramelised onion and smoked mozzarella with pesto or salsa bases. ◈ Map B5 • 1a Bedford St, Newtown • 9516 1568 • Open Tue–Sun • $

5 Vargabarespresso
A friendly Newtown café offers good breakfasts, burgers and coffee ◈ Map B5 • 10 Wilson St, Newtown • 9517 1932 • $

6 Green Gourmet
Vegan food has never tasted so good as at this Buddhist Chinese restaurant. Lunchtime yum cha is excellent. ◈ Map C5 • 115 King St, Newtown • 9519 5330 • $

7 Oscillate Wildly
From its name, a riff on The Smiths' paean to Oscar Wilde, to its snow-white interior, metal ceiling and eclectic oscillating menu, style and substance fuse beautifully in this temple to protein. ◈ Map B5 • 2/5 Australia St, Newtown • 9517 4700 • BYO • $$

8 Thanh Binh
Vietnamese food is great for meat lovers, who come here for a variety of pho: huge, comforting bowls of noodles and meatballs topped with mint leaves and broth. ◈ Map C5 • 111 King St, Newtown • 9557 1175 • BYO • $$

9 Badde Manors
Stop in to enjoy the bohemian charm of this busy café-cum-meeting spot, but expect haphazard service. ◈ Map C4 • 37 Globe Point Road, Globe • 9660 3797 • $

10 Flavour of India Glebe
The vegetarian dishes are the highlight here. Try a mix of daal and curries, and cut the spice with a cold mango lassi. ◈ Map K6 • 142a Glebe Point Rd, Glebe • 9692 0662 • BYO • $$

Lassi

Unless otherwise stated, all restaurants are open daily, accept credit cards, serve vegetarian meals, and provide disabled access.

107

Left **Handmade soaps at the Balmain Markets** Centre **Leichhardt Town Hall** Right **Italian Forum**

Balmain & Leichhardt

WILLIAM BALMAIN, *a surgeon on the First Fleet, was granted 223 ha (550 acres) west of the city in 1800, perhaps in gratitude for having tended to Governor Phillip following his 1790 spearing (see p38). The area was subdivided in the mid-1800s, and grand harbourside residences were erected alongside working-class stone and timber cottages and a multitude of pubs that catered to the employees of the local timber, mining and maritime industries. By the 1960s, Balmain had become a haven for writers, artists and actors, a reputation it still retains today.*

Balmain war memorial

Leichhardt's cultural connections are more tenuous. The suburb was named after the explorer Ludwig Leichhardt (see p79) who disappeared without a trace while crossing the continent in 1848; Patrick White (see p40) immortalised Leichhardt in his 1957 novel, Voss. Now Leichhardt is home to two diverse populations – Sydney's colourful "Little Italy" and a prominent lesbian community.

A café-junkshop in Balmain

🔟 Sights

1. Balmain East
2. Darling Street
3. Elkington Park
4. Birchgrove
5. Cockatoo Island
6. Goat Island
7. Leichhardt Town Hall
8. Leichhardt Post Office
9. Norton Street
10. Italian Forum

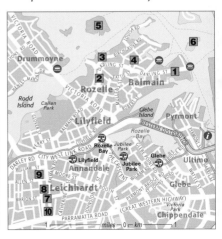

Share your travel recommendations on traveldk.com

Saturday Balmain Markets at St. Andrew's

Balmain East
At the eastern end of the Balmain peninsula is the Darling Point Wharf, overlooked by manicured Thornton Park. A sign tracing the route of the Balmain History Trail can be found near the bus stop. On Darling Street, check out the former Dolphin Hotel and the Waterman's Cottage. To the south, Peacock Point offers great views over Millers Point, Darling Harbour and the Anzac Bridge. Mort Bay Reserve to the north features two massive ships' propellers and views over the ferry and tugboat maintenance yards in Mort Bay. ◈ *Map C3*

Darling Street
Darling Street runs from the wharf in Balmain East to Victoria Road in Rozelle. It's a steady uphill climb from the wharf past narrow Victorian houses until you reach the friendly London Hotel, just before a large roundabout. En route you pass the childhood home of former New South Wales premier Neville Wran, No. 117, and the 1854 Watch House at No. 179, the oldest in Sydney. Find Gladstone Park past the roundabout, and St. Andrew's across the road, which hosts the Balmain Markets every Saturday. From here on it's boutiques, cafés, bookshops and salons all the way to the Victorian court house, Town Hall, Fire Station and Library *(see p57)*. ◈ *Map B3*

Elkington Park
This lovely reserve on White Horse Point, overlooking Cockatoo Island, is best known for the Dawn Fraser Pool, one of Sydney's oldest municipal pools. Dawn Fraser is a local legend, as much loved for her candid take on life and wild streak as she is for having dominated the pool at the 1956, 1960 and 1964 Olympic Games, leaving 40 world records in her wake. Although prone to tidal fluctuations, the pool is pleasantly unpretentious and a good place to strike up a conversation with an old-time local. ◈ *Map B2*

Birchgrove
This area has some lovely Colonial homes, a small shopping village on Rowntree Street and Birchgrove Park, the site of Australia's first Rugby League match in 1908. The northern tip of Birchgrove is known as Yurulbin Point, formerly called Long Nose Point, which, along with Manns Point, forms the mouth of the Parramatta River. Yurulbin Park has spectacular views of the Harbour Bridge, and an interpretation board near the ferry wharf provides interesting details on the area's Aboriginal heritage. ◈ *Map B2*

Spaghetti Western
When the first Italians escaped war-torn Europe to arrive in Leichhardt in 1917, the area was largely populated by Irish free settlers. After WWII many more Italians were drawn by the availability of paid work, fine weather and peace. The Italians, who continued to pour in until the 1960s, introduced Sydneysiders to many new things, perhaps most importantly espresso and spaghetti.

The Leichhardt area once belonged to the Wangal tribe of indigenous people.

Cockatoo Island

5 Since European settlement, the largest of Sydney Harbour's islands has been used variously as a convict prison, granary, girls reformatory and a major shipyard. Convicts from the infamous Norfolk Island penal colony were quartered on the island until 1871. During that time only one prisoner, the bushranger nicknamed "Captain Thunderbolt" escaped, aided by his Aboriginal wife, Mary. Sutherland Dock was completed in 1890 and the island became a major shipyard. It also served as the naval dockyard for the Royal Australian Navy at the outbreak of World War I. The dockyards closed down in 1992 and the Sydney Harbour Federation Trust has opened the island to the public. The trust runs activities, events and tours on the island *(see p15).* ◉ *Map B2*

Goat Island

6 Northeast of Balmain, Goat Island was one of Bennelong's *(see p9)* favourite picnic spots. In the 1830s it was used as a gunpowder magazine and convict barracks. One prisoner, Charles "Bony" Anderson, tried numerous times to escape the barracks, receiving 1,200 lashes for his troubles. He was chained to a sandstone "couch" for two years. The island later became a base for the Water Police and Fire Brigade, and in 1925 shipyards were built on its western side. In the 1990s it was the film set for the TV series *Water Rats*. Boasting fantastic views of Sydney Harbour, the island is managed by the National Parks and Wildlife Service *(see p14).* ◉ *Map C2*

Leichhardt Town Hall

Leichhardt Town Hall

7 Designed by Drake and Walcott and built in 1888, the style of this ornate building is described as Victorian Free Classical. The structure reflects the creativity and craftsmanship applied towards significant buildings of its time. When it opened, the Town Hall was considered the best municipal building outside the city centre. Many of the Italian migrants who settled in Leichhardt became Australian citizens in Town Hall ceremonies between 1920 and 1960. ◉ *Map A5 • 107 Norton St*

Leichhardt Post Office

8 Designed by James Barnet *(see p77),* Leichhardt Post Office is no longer in use, but it is possible to admire its strong lines and severe shape from the street. It is a good example of the Victorian Italianate style, popularised in Australia by architectural pattern books and used in many homes. The tower, designed to accommodate a clock that never arrived, provides a formal divide between the public and residential parts of the building. ◉ *Map A4 • 109 Norton St*

Leichhardt Post Office

There isn't much accommodation in Leichhardt, but if you're keen to stay in the area, try the Pensione Italia at 73 Renwick Street.

9 Norton Street

Named after James Norton, an English attorney who arrived in 1818 and established a thriving legal practice in the colony, Norton Street has long been the heart of this district. Much of the large estate purchased by Norton in 1834 is now the bustling shopping and dining strip that runs from Parramatta Road to Allen Street. You'll find a range of stores with an Italian flavour (see p62), from bridal fashion to books, clothing and shoes, as well as bakeries, delis and butchers. ◎ Map A4

10 Italian Forum

This kitsch development evokes reminiscences of Italy, and has a sundial and a statue of Dante based on a similar one in Verona. On the mezzanine level, you'll find boutiques selling imported and local Italian fashion. Descending the stairs finds the piazza, surrounded by cafés and restaurants that offer wonderful, sunny positions for languid lunches. Located on the piazza level is the Leichhardt Library which contains a Local History Section, a rich source of historical photographs and oral histories of the local Italian community. ◎ Map A5
• 23 Norton St • Leichhardt Library: open 9.30am–8pm Mon–Fri, 9:30am–4pm Sat, 10am–4pm Sun

Restaurant at the Italian Forum

A Balmain Stroll

Morning

🕙 Catch a ferry from **Circular Quay** (see p18) to the quaint **Darling Street Wharf**. Enter **Illoura Reserve** and walk south beneath she-oaks and other native trees to **Peacock Point**'s views across to **Darling Harbour** (see p28). Johnston Street has great views of **Anzac Bridge** (see p105). Head back to Darling Street and admire some of Balmain's finest residences. Turn into Killeen Street and wander down through **Ewenton Park**. Around the corner is grand **Hampton Villa** overlooking the docklands, home of Sir Henry Parkes (see p37). Back at Darling Street, get a drink at the pleasant **London Hotel**. Then, window-shop all the way to the **Town Hall**. Finally, backtrack to **Go Bungai** at 333 Darling Street for the best Japanese lunch in town.

Afternoon

After lunch, continue back down Darling Street to Mort Street and turn left. At the end is **Mort Bay Park**, site of the former Mort's Dock shipyards, named for Thomas Mort (see p79), which is now open harbourside parkland. Follow the shoreline around to the steps leading up to Wharf Road via Ronald Street. This lovely street leads to **Snails Bay** and the historic **Birchgrove Park**. A path traces the shoreline to Louisa Road, which has some seriously expensive real estate. Turn right and head towards **Yurulbin Park** for some spectacular harbour views before catching the ferry back to Circular Quay.

Around Town – Balmain & Leichhardt

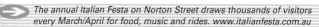

The annual Italian Festa on Norton Street draws thousands of visitors every March/April for food, music and rides. www.italianfesta.com.au

111

Interior and exterior of Welcome Hotel

🔟 Pubs & Bars

Commercial Hotel
1 You'll wish the second oldest pub in Balmain was your local after enjoying live music, couches to relax in and friendly owners behind the bar. ⊗ Map C3 • 82 Darling St, Balmain East • 9810 4195

London Hotel
2 Established in 1870, this is one of the most atmospheric pubs in Sydney. Grab a tractor seat on the balcony, sip the west Australian wheat bear, Red Back beer, and enjoy Harbour Bridge views. ⊗ Map C3 • 234 Darling St, Balmain • 9555 1377 • www.thelondonhotel.com.au

Welcome Hotel
3 The bistro at this Irish pub serves excellent food. Portions are generous and European flavours are infused with an Irish influence. ⊗ Map B3 • 91 Evans St, Rozelle • 9810 1323 • www.thewelcomehotel.com • $$

Town Hall Hotel
4 Something for everyone with great bar food, a giant screen, lounge area and discrete gaming section. It's the best place for a pick-me-up brunch. ⊗ Map B3 • 366 Darling St, Balmain • 9818 8950 • www.townhallhotel.com.au • Dis access

Riverview Hotel
5 This tiny local with much charm and fin-de-siècle interiors is hidden in a backstreet but is certainly worth seeking out. ⊗ Map B2 • 29 Birchgrove Rd, Balmain • 9810 1151

Sackville Hotel
6 A busy schedule of comedy, trivia and movie nights at this stylish pub, as well as live DJs. I also has an excellent and reasonably priced menu. ⊗ Map B3 • 599 Darling St, Rozelle • 9555 7555 • Dis access

Royal Hotel
7 An excellent local with entertainment every night, including a pool competition on Mondays. The place really comes alive on Friday and Saturday nights for karaoke sessions. ⊗ Map A4 • 156 Norton St, Leichhardt • 9569 2638 • www.royalhotelleichhardt.com

Martini
8 Upstairs in the Palace Cinema complex, pop in to sip martinis and mull over the latest flick. Fun atmosphere and tasty food. ⊗ Map A5 • Level 1, 99 Norton St Leichhardt • 9568 3344

Leichhardt Hotel
9 More a bar than a pub, with a feisty Italian crowd. In summer the doors fold back to make an outdoor party, and in winter gas heaters keep you snug. ⊗ Map A5 • 95 Norton St, Leichhardt • 9569 6640

Nortons on Norton
10 A traditional pub revamped with a restaurant and giant screens. The upper level has a clubby feel with DJs and pool tables. ⊗ Map A5 • 1 Norton St, Leichhardt • 9560 3322

Martini

Price Categories

For a two course meal for one with a drink (or equivalent meal), plus taxes and extra charges.

$	under $35
$$	$35–$60
$$$	$60–$120
$$$$	$120–$200
$$$$$	over $200

Fresh bread at Victoire

Best of the Rest

1 Elio
Great Italian food and friendly service. The soft hues and comfort food will make you feel warm inside. ◈ Map A4 • 159 Norton St, Leichhardt • 9560 9129 • Dis access • $$

2 Il Piave
A refined North Italian *cucina* turns out seasonal and regional delights. Head to the back courtyard. ◈ Map B3 • 639 Darling St, Rozelle • 9810 6204 • Open Tue–Sun • Bookings essential • $$

3 the barn café and grocery
You'll feel right at home here. Kids happily get their own menus, and adults get gourmet groceries to take away. ◈ Map B3 • 731-735 Darling St, Rozelle • 9810 1633 • $$

4 Blue Ginger
Modern Asian food from Thailand, Vietnam, China and Japan at great prices. There's something for everyone. ◈ Map C3 • 241 Darling St, Balmain • 9810 4005 • Bookings essential • Dis access • $

5 Victoire
Stop in for picnic supplies such as crusty sourdough bread and excellent cheese. ◈ Map B3 • 285 Darling St, Balmain • 9818 5529

6 Belle Fleur
Handcrafted chocolates and truffles, many with unusual flavours such as wattleseed and lemon myrtle, are exquisitely

Chocolate violin at Belle Fleur

decorated and boxed. ◈ Map B3 • 658 Darling St, Rozelle • 9810 2690

7 Berkelouw
At this wonderful book-store, take your tomes to the café upstairs and settle into a comfy couch. ◈ Map A5 • 70 Norton St, Leichhardt • 9560 3200

8 Palace Cinema
Catch the latest quality films at this small, stylish cinema. ◈ Map A5 • 99 Norton St, Leichhardt • 9550 0122

9 Alfie's Little Brother Carter
A neat shop sells the best local and imported streetwear. ◈ Map B3 • 348 Darling St, Balmain • 9555 5222

10 Rozelle Markets
The best Sydney market for vintage clothes and bric-a-brac. ◈ Map B3 • Rozelle Public School, Darling St, Rozelle • Every Sat & Sun • 9818 5373

The Palace Norton St Cinema offers mothers and babies sessions called "Babes in Arms" at 11am every Thursday.

Around Town – Balmain & Leichhardt

Left **Decorative gables at Manly** Center **Manly Beach** Right **Detail on New Brighton Hotel**

The North Shore

IF THE EASTERN SUBURBS ARE *"gorgeous"*, and the southern and western suburbs are *"aspirational"*, the North Shore is best described as *"satisfied"*. For many Sydneysiders the North Shore is not only geographical shorthand for the suburbs north of the harbour, it's equally a state of mind. One that is respectable, well-off and content. From Hunters Hill in the west to Manly in the east, and all points north to Ku-ring-gai Chase National Park, the North Shore is bourgeois to the back teeth. Here you'll find some glorious pockets of remnant bushland nestled around the harbour, stunning ocean beaches,

A giraffe at Taronga Zoo

quiet harbourside beaches, and plenty of options for those who love the great outdoors, walking, cycling, kayaking, surfing, diving, sailing and parasailing. And then there are always some of Sydney's perennial favourites to tempt you: Luna Park, Nutcote, Taronga Park Zoo, Bradleys Head, Oceanworld Manly and North Head.

Sights

1. Balls Head Reserve
2. Lavender Bay & Blues Point
3. Milsons Point
4. North Sydney
5. Kirribilli
6. Neutral Bay & Cremorne
7. Mosman & Balmoral
8. Middle Harbour
9. Manly
10. Manly Scenic Walk

Mural on a surf shop

Balls Head Reserve

On the headland east of Manns Point and the Parramatta River *(see p109)* lies this pleasant park, site of Aboriginal rock art and bushwalking trails. It offers stunning views across the harbour to Goat Island *(see p110)* and Balmain *(see p108)*. BBQ facilities are available, and it's easily accessible from Waverton Railway Station. The park is cradled by the dormitory suburbs of Waverton and Wollstoncraft, the latter named after Edward Wollstoncraft, nephew of Mary Wollstoncraft, the author of *Rights of Women*. Edward was an enterprising local merchant who operated a shipping business with his partner Alexander Berry, after whom the bay was named. ⊗ *Map C2*

Lavender Bay & Blues Point

East of Berry's Bay, this cove has great views of the Opera House framed by the Harbour Bridge. It was named after George Lavender, a boatswain who married the daughter of his neighbour Billy Blue *(see p37)*. In 1817 Governor Macquarie granted Billy Blue 32 ha (80 acres) west of Lavender Bay. In 1830, at the age of 82, Billy Blue established a ferry service from Dawes Point *(see p13)* to the headland that now bears his name. There is a small reserve at its end, but the point is dominated by a Harry Seidler *(see p47)* apartment building that many consider an eyesore. ⊗ *Map D2*

Milsons Point

Nestled beneath the Harbour Bridge is a tiny suburb best known for its fun fair. Luna Park *(see p56)*, which is based on New York's Coney Island. Luna

Crowds at Luna Park, Milsons Point

Park's famous laughing clown face set between two Art Deco towers, although remodelled several times over the years, has continuously overlooked the harbour since 1935. The park is built upon a former Sydney Harbour Bridge construction wharf and workshops. Beside the park is the North Sydney Olympic Pool *(see p49)* which opened in 1936. ⊗ *Map D2*

North Sydney

In 1932 John Bradfield *(see p12)* predicted that, with the opening of the Harbour Bridge, North Sydney and Mosman would merge into a second Brooklyn. He was certainly on the money regarding North Sydney's development, as indicated by the area's many skyscrapers. Sydney's second CBD is home to major Australian banking, finance and insurance giants. Its attractions include a small museum, chapel and tomb dedicated to the memory and works of Australia's only saint, Mary MacKillop (1842–1909), who was beatified in 1995. ⊗ *Map D1* • *Mary MacKillop Place Museum: 7 Mount St* • *8912 4878* • *www.marymackillopplace.org.au* • *Open 10am–4pm daily* • *Adm*

Apartments at Kirribilli

Kirribilli

Kirribilli is Australia's most densely populated suburb. But it is better known for two residences that occupy its tip: Admiralty House (1843) and neighbouring Kirribilli House (1855). The former was the residence of the Commander of the British Royal Navy, and is now the Sydney residence of the Governor General, the Queen's representative in Australia. The latter is the official Sydney residence of the Australian Prime Minister. The Gothic Kirribilli House has one of the best views in Australia. Map D2

Neutral Bay & Cremorne

Neutral Bay was named by Governor Phillip, who ordered that all foreign ships entering Sydney Harbour anchor here. The area includes Careening Cove, so named because ships were laid on their sides here for refitting. Now this tranquil bay is home to the Royal Sydney Yacht Squadron, the Ensemble Theatre (see p65), and the Sydney Flying Squadron. May Gibbs' (see p40) residence, Nutcote, is on the eastern slope. Further east is Cremorne, a long, narrow peninsula with a popular harbourside reserve. Map D1
• Nutcote: 5 Wallaringa Ave, Neutral Bay
• 9953 4453 • www.maygibbs.com.au
• Open 11am–3pm Wed–Sun • Adm

Mosman & Balmoral

Mosman Bay was named after Archibald Mosman, who established a whaling business nearby in 1830. The suburb is best known for Taronga Zoo (see p32–3) and Bradleys Head (see p50). Lieutenant William Bradley arrived with the First Fleet and later served in the Napoleonic Wars, before he was found guilty of fraud and exiled to France in 1814. Headland Park, unites the former military lands at Chowder Bay, Georges Heights and Middle Head, offers harbourside walking tracks and several restaurants. Balmoral (see p48) has three beaches, including Chinaman's Beach. Map F1

Middle Harbour

The entrance to the northern arm of the harbour is marked by Middle Head and Dobroyd Head. North of Chinaman's Beach is the Spit Bridge, which can be raised allowing boats to pass beneath. Castlecrag, northwest of the Spit Bridge, was home for a period to Walter Burley Griffin (1876–1937), the US architect who designed Australia's capital, Canberra. Much of Middle Harbour's shoreline is parkland, with calm waters perfect for kayaking (see p54). To the north is Garigal National Park (see p50). Map T3

> ### Krishnamurti's Amphitheatre
>
> An amphitheatre was built in Balmoral in 1924 by Theosophists who anticipated a Second Coming under their spiritual leader, Jiddu Krishnamurti (1897–1986). This structure was one of several worldwide dedicated to the "World Teacher", who had been discovered as a boy in Madras. Krishnamurti renounced the Theosophists in 1929.

Mosman's Military Road contains the best shops for picnic supplies, gifts, cheese, chocolates, seafood and more.

Walking along Manly Beach

9 Manly

This peninsula was so named because Governor Phillip felt the Aborigines he met here in 1788 were "manly". In 1853, businessman Henry Smith purchased 121 ha (300 acres) on the formerly remote peninsula, and set about creating a seaside pleasure resort. Today, Manly is a very popular and lively destination. Home to lovely beaches, it also features attractions such as Oceanworld Manly (see p118) and October's Manly Jazz Festival (see p73). Catch the enjoyable harbour ferry ride from Circular Quay and make a full day of it (see p39).

⊗ *Manly Visitor Information Centre: The Forecourt, Manly Wharf • 9976 1430 • Open 9am–5pm Mon–Fri, 10am–4pm Sat, Sun & public holidays*

10 Manly Scenic Walk

A 10-km (6-mile) walk, one of Sydney's best, traces North Harbour's shoreline from Manly to the Spit Bridge. The walk passes by coastal heathlands, flat sandy beaches and sub-tropical rainforest. Highlights on the way include pretty Forty Baskets Beach, rugged Dobroyd Head, the 1911 Grotto Point Lighthouse, Clontarf Beach (see p48), and Aboriginal shell middens east of the Spit Bridge. The NPWS (see p14) offers a useful map of the route, available at the NPWS and Manly Visitor Information Centres.

A Beach Crawl Around Manly

Morning

Pack the bare essentials and catch the ferry to Manly Wharf. Cross **The Esplanade** and follow **The Corso** down to **Manly Beach** (see p118). After paying homage to William Gocher (see p39), head south and follow the path around to **Cabbage Tree Bay**, where you'll find the delightful **Fairy Bower** rockpool and **Shelly Beach** (see p118), both of which are perfect for children. Then extract your credit card and enjoy lunch at the classy **Le Kiosk** (see p119), voted the most romantic restaurant on the East Coast by the *New York Times*.

Afternoon

Leave the beach via Bower Street and follow this around to College Street, past the million-dollar mansions overlooking Manly Beach. Turn right into Reddall Street, left into Addison Road, and left again into Darley Road. Head uphill and take a peek over the stone walls at the **Former St Patrick's Seminary** (see p118). Continue past the hospital and take the right fork leading into **Sydney Harbour National Park** (see p14). Pass beneath the sandstone arch and take Collins Beach Road on your right. This winds down through a lovely shaded gully to the **Police College**. A small path on your right leads to the secluded **Collins Beach** (see p38), one of Sydney's hidden secrets. A path at the end of the beach leads to Stuart Street, which takes you back to Manly.

Left **Oceanworld** Centre **Shelly Beach** Right **Former St Patrick's Seminary**

TOP 10 Manly

1 Manly Cove
The ferry wharf houses boutiques and cafés, a Visitor Information Centre *(see p117)*, Manly Boat and Kayak Hire, Oceanworld and the Manly Art Gallery and Museum. ⊗ *Map U3 • Manly Boat and Kayak Hire: 0412 622 662 • Manly Art Gallery and Museum: 9976 1420*

Brass band at The Corso

2 Oceanworld Manly
Dive with sharks, giant turtles and rays on Oceanworld's Shark Dive Xtreme. For the less courageous there are live shows and guided tours. Passes allow multiple entry. ⊗ *Map U3 • West Esplanade • 8251 7877 • Open 10am–5:30pm daily • www.oceanworld.com.au • Adm*

3 The Corso
This lively pedestrian avenue runs from The Esplanade to Manly Beach. The Manly Deli is a good place to stock up for a picnic lunch. ⊗ *Map U3*

4 New Brighton Hotel
Built in 1926, this Egyptian Classical Revival Style pub on The Corso is a popular summer watering hole. ⊗ *Map U3*

5 Manly Beach
Backed by a reserve lined with Norfolk Island pines and a busy esplanade, this ocean beach *(see p48)* is a Sydney favourite. There are rock baths at the northern end. ⊗ *Map U3*

6 Cabbage Tree Bay
A lovely bay that features shallow crystal waters, wind-sculpted sandstone cliffs, the magical Fairy Bower rockpool and protected Shelly Beach. ⊗ *Map U3*

7 Former St Patrick's Seminary
A prominent 1885 seminary for Catholic priests was the setting for Thomas Keneally's *(see p41)* novel *Three Cheers for the Paraclete*. It is now a college of hospitality and tourism. ⊗ *Map U3*

8 North Head
This windswept, heath-covered highlight of the Sydney Harbour National Park *(see p14)* is home to the former North Fort Artillery Museum. The museum has re-opened as an ecological sanctuary. ⊗ *Map U3 • 8969 2100 for museum information)*

9 Old Quarantine Station
Until 1984, Sydney's infected arrivals were quarantined at this bulwark against infectious diseases. ⊗ *Map U3 • North Head, Sydney Harbour National Park*

10 Collins Beach
The site where Governor Phillip was speared in 1788 is a peaceful spot nowadays *(see p38)*. Steps lead to a secluded rock diving platform.

Price Categories
For a two course meal
for one with a drink
(or equivalent meal),
plus taxes and extra
charges.

$ under $35
$$ $35–$60
$$$ $60–$120
$$$$ $120–$200
$$$$$ over $200

TOP 10 Places to Eat

Around Town – The North Shore

1 Nilgiri's
A low-key Indian restaurant with a small, well-chosen menu. On Sunday they have regional buffets for lunch and dinner. They also offer private cushion rooms and cooking classes. ✆ Map T3
• 81 Christie St, St Leonards • 9966 0636
• www.nilgiris.com.au • $$

2 Mosman Rowers
This club is a short walk from Mosman Bay wharf. The views from the balcony are spectacular. ✆ Map F1 • 3 Centenary Ave, Mosman Bay • 9953 7966
• www.mosmanrowers.com.au • $$

3 Sushi Studio
Authentic and traditional Japanese food. Sit at the sushi bar and order a deluxe plate to witness the chef's slicing prowess. ✆ Map E1 • 75 Military Rd, Neutral Bay • 9953 7317 • No dis access • $

4 Orso
Located on the beach, Orso directly overlooks Middle Harbour through its full-length glass windows. The seafood platter for two or more is great value. ✆ Map U3 • 79 Parriwi Rd, The Spit, Mosman • 9968 3666
• www.orso.com.au • $$$

5 Confiseur & Co
Mosman has wonderful food shops and delicatessens. This bakery and patisserie offers pots of tea, savoury pies and sweet treats. ✆ Map U3 • 840 Military Rd, Mosman • 9969 4599 • $

6 Out of Africa
You don't need a safari suit to indulge in North African delicacies, such as tagines, while leaning back against the zebra-skin banquettes. Map U3 • 43–45 East Esplanade, Manly • 9977 0055 • www.outofafrica.com.au • No dis access • $$

7 Le Kiosk
Saunter around the bay from Manly Beach to Le Kiosk, where it's all about location. It looks like a beach house but has serious food. Request a table on the veranda. ✆ Map U3 • Shelly Beach
• 9977 4122 • www.lekiosk.com.au • $$$

8 Ocean Foods
On a sunny day, nothing beats eating fish and chips on the beach. Get your fish grilled and a healthy salad on the side – and don't feed the seagulls. ✆ Map U3 • The Corso, Manly • 9977 1059 • No dis access • $

9 Gelatissimo
The best choice for an ice cream craving. Standards and exotic flavours are topped with chunks of chocolate, piles of figs or handfuls of almonds. ✆ Map U3 • Kiosk 2, Manly Wharf, Manly • 9976 6199
• www.gelatissimo.com.au • No dis access

10 Crows Nest Plaza
This little shopping mall has a clutch of good, cheap diners serving Himalayan, Japanese, Indian and Singaporean cuisines. ✆ Map T3 • 103–11 Willoughby Rd, Crows Nest • No dis access • $

Unless otherwise stated, all restaurants are open daily, accept credit cards, serve vegetarian meals, and provide disabled access.

Grose Valley from Govetts Leap, considered the best view of the Blue Mountains

Beyond Sydney

THE REGION SURROUNDING SYDNEY *offers a wealth of natural attractions, historic towns and villages, restaurants with million-dollar views, and endless options for outdoor activities. All regions covered in this section are accessible by public transport, but hiring a car will give you far greater flexibility. To the north of Sydney is Ku-ring-gai Chase National Park, the Hawkesbury River, the Central Coast and Hunter Valley. To the west are the famous Blue Mountains and historic Parramatta and Windsor, while to the south is the gorgeous Royal National Park and the Southern Highlands. All are only a day's trip away from Sydney, but try combining neighbouring attractions into an overnight or weekend trip, for each area offers a diverse and unique range of attractions. There are plenty of accommodation options, ranging from luxury guesthouses in the Blue Mountains to houseboats on the Hawkesbury River to beach campsites at the Royal National Park.*

Berrima, a Georgian village in the Southern Highlands

10 Attractions

1. Blue Mountains
2. Hunter Valley
3. Central Coast
4. Hawkesbury River
5. Pittwater & Broken Bay
6. Ku-ring-gai Chase National Park
7. Northern Beaches
8. Parramatta
9. Royal National Park
10. Southern Highlands

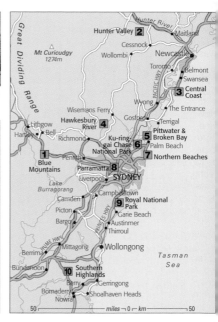

Sign up for DK's email newsletter on traveldk.com

Left **Rothbury Estate winery in Hunter Valley** Right **The picturesque Hawkesbury River**

1 Blue Mountains

These World Heritage-listed mountains are named for their constant bluish haze, the result of evaporating eucalyptus oil. The lovely mountains offer numerous bushwalks and plenty of natural attractions, including the Three Sisters, the Jenolan Caves and Wentworth Falls *(see p126)*. When the explorers Gregory Blaxland, William Lawson and WC Wentworth *(see p37)*, crossed the 1,100-m (3,600-ft) range in 1813, they opened up the continent's grassland interior to white settlement. The main township of Katoomba *(see p128)* is about 107 km (56 miles) west of Sydney.

2 Hunter Valley

Grapes have been grown in this region since the 1830s. Now there are more than 60 vineyards and countless providores producing condiments, cheese and other gourmet delicacies; some also contain restaurants or cafés. Most of the wineries surround Pokolbin and neighbouring Cessnock, which is the regional township closest to Sydney. Beautiful Hunter Valley is also a popular area for outdoor activities such as cycling, golf, horseriding and hot air ballooning. Numerous tour operators in Sydney offer attractive day, overnight and weekend packages to the area.

3 Central Coast

The coast from Broken Bay *(see p122)* to Newcastle offers glorious ocean beaches, national parks and several lakes and water-ways. The main regional town is Gosford, at the head of Brisbane Water. This large waterway runs out to Broken Bay past Woy Woy and the pleasant townships of Hardy's Bay in Killcare, Pretty Beach and Wagstaffe. Behind Wagstaffe is Bouddi National Park *(see p127)*, which extends north to pleasant McMaster's Beach. Pearl Beach *(see p128)* and the tiny fishing village of Patonga, surrounded by Brisbane Water National Park *(see p127)*, overlook Broken Bay. ◈ *Map U1*

4 Hawkesbury River

This broad river runs from Windsor *(see p124)* in the west to Broken Bay *(see p122)* in the east, passing massive sandstone escarpments, historic riverside towns, national parks, mangrove islands, fishing villages and holiday homes, as well as the spectacular Berowa Waters and Cowan Creek *(see p128)* coves and Pittwater *(see p122)*. Berowa Waters is home to the famous Berowa Waters Inn. Cowan Creek peters out near pretty Bobbin Head. Although parts of the river are popular with water-skiers, it's actually best enjoyed at a leisurely pace. ◈ *Map U1*

Palm Beach peninsula's Whale Beach

5 Pittwater & Broken Bay

Pittwater is a long, slender waterway running from Newport to Palm Beach *(see p48)*, Ku-ring-gai Chase National Park and Broken Bay. Exclusive houses, private wharves and public marinas populate its eastern shoreline. Housing on the western shoreline thins out as you head north, until you reach Ku-ring-gai Chase National Park, north of isolated Towlers Bay and exclusive Scotland Island. Pittwater's sheltered waters have long been a favourite haunt with yachties. Broken Bay is a beautiful, wide and sometimes wild expanse of water dominated by Lion Island, an uninhabited rocky outcrop. ◈ *Map U1*

6 Ku-ring-gai Chase National Park

Bounded by the Hawkesbury River to the north and Pittwater to the east, this gorgeous native bushland is a bushwalker's and kayaker's delight. There are numerous walking trails, picnic areas, The Basin campsite, lookouts, hundreds of Aboriginal rock art sites, secluded beaches, a tucked-away restaurant overlooking the water at Cottage Point and marinas at Akuna Bay and Bobbin Head. Cycling and horseriding are allowed in certain sections of the park. Flora and fauna highlights include banksias, waratahs, Sydney red gums, wallabies, flying foxes, pelicans, platypus, blue-tongued lizards, cockatoos and parrots. The information centre runs activities and provides maps and useful tips. ◈ *Map T1*
• *Information Centre: via Bobbin Head • 9472 8949*
• *Open 10am–4pm daily*

Rock art at Ku-ring-gai Chase National Park

7 Northern Beaches

This stretch of stunning ocean beaches runs from Manly to Barrenjoey Head. Palm Beach *(see p48)* is a haven for Sydney millionaires, as well as being the outdoor location for the popular TV soap opera *Home and Away*. The Barrenjoey Lighthouse over-looks Broken Bay, the Central Coast and the Hawkesbury River *(see p121)*. Behind Palm Beach lies lovely Pittwater. ◈ *Map U1*

8 Parramatta

The fertile soil found here in the 1780s spared the fledgling colony from probable starvation and spawned Sydney's original satellite township. It was a rural retreat for Governor Phillip, who built a cottage here in 1790. Old Government House *(see p125)*, which replaced Phillip's cottage in 1799, is one of Sydney's most historic sites. Other highlights include Experiment Farm Cottage, Elizabeth Farm, Hambledon Cottage *(see pp124–5)* and Australia's oldest cemetery, St. John's. Here you'll find the grave of "The Flogging Parson", Reverend Samuel Marsden, the early colony's notoriously sadistic magistrate. ◈ *Map S3 • St. John's Cemetery: O'Connell St, Parramatta*

Royal National Park

9 Proclaimed in 1879, this is Australia's oldest national park and the world's second oldest. The 15,074-ha (37,248-acre) park is 32 km (19 miles) south of Sydney. Here you'll find subtropical rainforests, deep valleys, cycle and walking trails, rugged ocean beaches, sandstone clifftops, heathlands, mangroves and inland lagoons. There are several picnic- and campgrounds, and if you're lucky you could spy a swamp wallaby, a satin bowerbird, a pied oystercatcher or the endangered tiger quoll. A tram from Loftus Station connects with the visitors centre on Sundays and public holidays.

Waratah

⦿ *Map S6 • Visitors Centre: Farnell Ave, Audley Heights • 9542 0648 • Open 9.30am–4:30pm Mon–Fri, 8:30am–4:30pm Sat–Sun and public holidays*

Southern Highlands

10 The coastal hinterland and the city of Wollongong, one or two hours south of Sydney, is a popular weekend getaway destination. With no shortage of antiques and crafts shops, galleries, B&Bs, English-style pubs, ivy-clad Georgian buildings and cottage gardens, this region is reminiscent of the English countryside. Since 1993, a major attraction has been Bundanon, the former estate and studio of artist Arthur Boyd, who bequeathed his property to the nation. Other popular attractions include the historic townships of Bowral *(see p125)*, Berrima, Kiama *(see p127)*, Berry and Kangaroo Valley. The movie *Babe* was filmed in nearby Robertson.

A Scenic Drive by Hawkesbury River

Morning

🕒 Head north across the **Harbour Bridge** and follow the signs to **Windsor** *(see p124)*. After a pit stop at the 1815 **Macquarie Arms Hotel** on George Street, backtrack to Pitt Town Road and follow this northwards. It becomes Cattai Road and then the Wisemans Ferry Road, passing through farmland and bush before dropping down to Wisemans Ferry on the **Hawkesbury River** *(see p121)*. Take the southern ferry across the Hawkesbury and follow the incredibly scenic road that tracks the **Macdonald River** as far as **St Albans** *(see p124)*, where you can enjoy lunch at the 1848 **Settlers Arms Inn**.

Afternoon

Head back towards Wisemans Ferry along the other side of the Macdonald River until it meets the Hawkesbury River. Follow the river beneath its sandstone escarpments and through the isolated riverside townships of **Gunderman** and **Spencer** before climbing up through the forest to **Central Mangrove**. Drop down to **Calga** via Peats Ridge and take the Old Pacific Highway south to the Hawkesbury again. Cross the river and take the turnoff to the small fishing and boating township of **Brooklyn**. Enjoy an ale at the **Anglers Rest Hotel** or take a 15-minute ferry trip across to Dangar Island's idyllic **Island Shop** for homemade cake and coffee over looking the water.

Around Town – Beyond Sydney

Left **Settlers Arms Inn, St Albans** Centre **Elizabeth Farm garden** Right **Hambledon Cottage**

TOP 10 Historic Sites & Townships

1 Windsor

Governor Macquarie established five towns in 1810 on the fertile land around the upper Hawkesbury River, one of which was Windsor, now a weekend tourist haven. The town's wonderful Colonial buildings include one of Australia's oldest pubs, the 1815 Macquarie Arms Hotel, as well as the 1823 St Mathew's Anglican Church and Rectory, designed by Francis Greenway *(see p23)*.

Macquarie Arms Hotel, Windsor

2 Rouse Hill House and Farm

Richard Rouse (1774–1852), Superintendent of Public Works and Convicts at Parramatta, once occupied this estate and was succeeded by seven generations of descendants. The 1813 Historic Houses Trust property features a Georgian residence, outbuildings and gardens. The furniture dates from the 1830s to the 1960s.
⊗ *Guntawong Rd, Rouse Hill • 9627 6777 • Open 9:30am–4:30pm Wed–Sun • Adm; guided tours only • Bookings advisable*

3 St Albans

The highlight of this quaint historical village is the charming Settlers Arms Inn. Built by convict labour between 1836 and 1848, this National Trust-classified pub overlooks the Macdonald River and offers good food and accommodation. ⊗ *Settlers Arms Inn: 1 Wharf St • www.settlersarms.com.au*

4 Experiment Farm Cottage

Emancipated convicts James and Elizabeth Ruse established Australia's first self-sufficient farm in 1789. In the colony's first land grant, Governor Phillip gave them a further 12 ha (30 acres) for their efforts. The charming Colonial bungalow was built by the farm's next owner, the surgeon John Harris. The property is owned by the National Trust. ⊗ *Map S4 • 9 Ruse St, Harris Park • 9635 5655 • Open 10:30am–3:30pm Tue–Fri (from 11am Sat–Sun) • Adm • www.nsw.nationaltrust.org.au*

5 Elizabeth Farm

Built by John and Elizabeth Macarthur *(see p37)*, this 1793 estate was once an important social, political and cultural centre. The farm's cottage is the oldest surviving building in Australia, and is carefully furnished with reproductions of the original interiors. ⊗ *Map S4 • 70 Alice St, Rosehill • 9635 9488 • Open 9:30am–4pm Fri–Sun • Adm • www.hht.net.au*

1810 medicine chest at Experiment Farm

Drawing room at Old Government House

6 Hambledon Cottage
Close by Elizabeth Farm, this cottage was named after a village in Hampshire, England. The Macarthurs built this cottage in 1824 as a retirement home for their governess, Penelope Lucas. The furnishings of the rendered sandstone cottage reflect the 1820s to the 1850s. ॐ *Map S3 • 63 Hassall St, Parramatta • 9635 6924 • Open 11am–4pm Wed, Thur, Sat & Sun • Adm*

7 Old Government House
Overlooking the Parramatta River, this distinguished plastered brick residence *(see p39)* is located on 105 ha (260 acres) of parkland and is owned by the National Trust. Australia's oldest public building, it was built by Governors Hunter and Macquarie between 1799 and 1818. The porch is credited to Francis Greenway. The interior faithfully reflects the Macquaries' era, and houses one of Australia's finest collections of 19th-century furniture. Tours explore the people who lived here as well as the eras they lived in. ॐ *www.nsw.nationaltrust.org.au*

8 Rock Art in Ku-ring-gai Chase National Park
Prior to white settlement, the area from Broken Bay to Sydney Harbour was inhabited by the Guringai people. However, by the 1840s, most had been wiped out by smallpox or driven away. Over 800 sites record the Aboriginal culture and their bond with the land, including rock engravings, axe-grinding grooves, burial sites, cave shelters, middens (sea-shell mounds) and ochre hand stencils. ॐ *Map T1*

9 Norman Lindsay Gallery
Artist and writer Norman Lindsay (1879–1969), much loved for his 1918 classic children's book *The Magic Pudding* and his paintings and sculptures of satyrs, nymphs and sirens, occupied this Blue Mountains property from 1912 until his death. The National Trust property is now a museum and gallery with an extensive collection of Lindsay's work, including novels, watercolours and sculptures. The main house, studios and pleasure gardens are all open to the public. ॐ *14 Norman Lindsay Crescent, Faulconbridge • 4751 1067 • Open 10am–4pm daily • Adm • www.normanlindsay.com.au*

10 Bowral
The Southern Highlands' main town began life in the 1860s when John Oxley, an early Colonial explorer, subdivided his land grant and a small township emerged. Home to an increasing number of urban refugees, Bowral has an arty, old-world feel, making it a popular and relaxing weekend destination for Sydneysiders. It is probably best known as the former home of the famous cricketer Sir Donald Bradman *(see p92)*.

Antiques shop in Bowral

The Three Sisters in the Blue Mountains

TOP 10 Natural Attractions

Jenolan Caves

1 Jenolan Caves

Discovered in 1838, this striking complex of underground limestone caves lies southwest of Katoomba *(see p128)* in the Blue Mountains *(see p121)*. They are Australia's best-known caves, renowned for their icy underground rivers, huge caverns and intriguing limestone formations, all surrounded by an extensive wildlife reserve.

2 Mount Annan Botanic Gardens

On display at this amazing Botanic Garden is 404ha (1000 acres) of Australian plant life. Drive through gardens displaying the bizarre and colourful plants that make their home on the great southern continent. On the hillsides, near the lakes and among the plants there is an abundance of bird life. Kangaroos can also be seen here. ◈ *Mt Annan Drive, Mt Annan • 4648 2477 • Open Apr–Sep: 10–4pm daily; Oct–Mar: 10am–6pm daily • Adm*

3 Three Sisters

The most popular landmark of the Blue Mountains is this spectacular rock formation, which derives its name from an Aboriginal Dreamtime legend. The story relates that the leader of the Gundungurra people, concerned for the safety of his three beautiful daughters, turned them into stone to protect them from enemies but died before being able to reverse his spell. The Three Sisters stand at the entrance to the long climb into Jamison Valley.

4 Wentworth Falls

These impressive 300-m (1,082-ft) falls mark the start of some of the Blue Mountains' most challenging walking trails down to neighbouring Jamison Valley. The Wentworth Falls Reserve lies near the village of Wentworth, named for one of the first Europeans to explore the region *(see p37)*.

Wentworth Falls

Mount Tomah Botanic Gardens

5 Kiama Blowhole

A large fishing and resort town, Kiama is one of the most attractive coastal spots south of Sydney. Discovered by explorer George Bass in 1797, this 25-m (82-ft) blowhole originates in a natural fault in the cliffs. It erupts whenever a wave hits with enough force, which can be every few minutes. Water can be thrown as high as 60 m (200 ft).

6 Illawarra Coast

A massive sandstone escarpment traces the coastline south of Royal National Park and north of Wollongong. A string of small towns nestled beneath the escarpment all offer spectacular ocean views.

7 Mount Tomah Botanic Gardens

Covering 28 ha (60 acres), these alpine gardens are located on a summit of the Blue Mountains. The rich basalt soil lies 1,000 m (3,281 ft) above sea level. Along with stunning views, the gardens feature an excellent collection of cool-climate plants. To reach the gardens, follow the Botanists' Way trail into the Blue Mountains. Ⓢ *Bells Line of Road via Bilpin • 4567 2154 • Open Mar–Oct: 10am–4pm daily; Oct–Mar: 10am–5pm daily • Adm*

8 Bouddi National Park

With clifftop walks overlooking the ocean and Broken Bay, secluded beaches, heathlands and banksia forests, this tiny coastal park is a gem. It extends from Box Head to McMaster's Beach on the Central Coast *(see p121)*, and offers good bushwalking trails and camping facilities. Ⓢ *NPWS: 207 Albany St North, Gosford • 4320 4200*

9 Wollemi National Park

This scenic national park is the largest wilderness area in NSW at 492,976 ha (1,217, 650 acres). The rugged terrain is composed of a maze of canyons and gorges that traverse rainforested mountains. Other features include riverside beaches, whitewater rafting and camping.

10 Brisbane Water National Park

Aboriginal rock art and spring wildflowers are the highlights of this 12,000-ha (39,640-acre) park overlooking Broken Bay and the Hawkesbury River. There are great views over the Hawkesbury from the path leading from Pearl Beach to tiny Patonga, accessible by ferry from Palm Beach *(see p48)*. Ⓢ *Map I11*

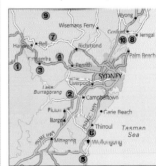

Left **Yachts in a creek at Pittwater** Centre **Palm Beach** Right **Seaplane at Rose Bay**

TOP 10 Things to Do

1 Swim at Pearl Beach
This National Trust hamlet is cradled by Brisbane Water National Park *(see p127)*. The calm waters and rockpool are simply magical. *Map U1*

2 Sail Pittwater & Cowan Creek
Hire a yacht and pack a picnic lunch to explore these isolated coves. *Map U1 • Hardy's Bay Yacht Charters: 46 Fisherman's Pde, Daleys Point • 4360 1442 • www.hbyc.com.au*

3 Hitch a Ride with the Riverboat Postman
Join this unique postal service as it delivers mail to isolated Hawkesbury River settlements. *Map T1 • Riverboat Postman: Dangar Rd, Brooklyn • 9985 7566 • 9:30am– 1:15pm Mon–Fri • Adm*

4 Surf at Palm Beach
There may be better waves to the south, but it's hard to beat the setting. *Map U1*

5 Seaplane to Lunch
For a romantic lunch, take a seaplane from Rose Bay *(see p17)* to the Cottage Point Inn restaurant on Cowan Creek, or enjoy a picnic at Pittwater.

6 Waratah Park Earth Sanctuary
See koalas, kangaroos, wombats and wallabies at this large bushland sanctuary. Downunder Experience offers tours. *Map T2 • 13 Namba Rd, Duffys Forest • 9986 1788 • www.waratahpark.com.au*

7 Visit Katoomba
Katoomba is the site of Echo Point, which offers superb views. Take a bushwalk around the clifftop paths or head down the Giant Stairway, across Jamison Valley *(see p126)* and back up on the Scenic Railway. *Echo Point Visitors Centre: Echo Point Road, Katoomba • 1300 653 408*

8 Overnight Trip to Canberra
Highlights of Australia's capital include the Parliament Houses, the National Gallery, the War Memorial, the National Library, Lake Burley Griffin and Black Mountain.

9 Southern Highlands
A quaint English-village feel permeates towns such as Bowral and Mittagong. Their main streets are lined with tea-houses and antiques shops.

10 Premier's Walk
Bob Carr, the NSW premier, is a Coast Track enthusiast. This 26-km (16-mile) route through the Royal National Park *(see p123)* offers ocean views and seasonal glimpses of migrating whales. You can walk a section of the track or go for the whole two-day stretch.

Kangaroo

Price Categories

For a two course meal	**$** under $35
for one with a drink	**$$** $35–$60
(or equivalent meal),	**$$$** $60–$120
plus taxes and extra	**$$$$** $120–$200
charges.	**$$$$$** over $200

Solitary

TOP 10 Places to Eat

1 The Roxy
A wonderful 1930 Spanish-Mission cinema is now a stylish complex with two bars, a theatre for gigs and a Thai restaurant, the Realm Restaurant. ◎ *Map S3 • 69 George St, Parramatta • 9687 4221 • Realm Restaurant: 9633 3790 • $*

2 Surfeit
Stop in at this café/food store to stock up on treats for a picnic. Try the rolls and risotto balls. ◎ *Map T6 • Shop 8, 2 Surf Rd, Cronulla • 9523 3873 • $*

3 Letterbox Restaurant
Tasty Mod Oz food in a delightful converted post office. For a true comfort meal, try the saltimbocca with grilled polenta. ◎ *4 Ash St, Terrigal • 4385 4222 • Open Tue–Sun, Mon group bookings only • No dis access • $$$*

4 Solitary
Serving modern Australian food often made with ingredients from its own organic garden, Solitary offers warm service and a beautiful view of the Jamison Valley. ◎ *90 Cliff Drive, Leura Falls • 4782 1164 • Open Wed–Sun • $$$*

5 Esca Bimbadgen
Let the staff match the winery's delicious Bimbadgen wines to your selection from the tasty Moz Oz menu. ◎ *790 McDonalds Rd, Pokolbin • 4998 4666 • $$$*

6 Paragon
Get a sense of Katoomba in its heyday at this atmospheric Art Deco café. Sit snug in a booth, choose from handmade chocolates on display, and be sure to check out the lovely back rooms. ◎ *65 Katoomba St, Katoomba • 4782 2928 • No dis access • $$*

7 The Chairman & Yip
Long considered one of Canberra's best restaurants, with a good value, modern Asian fusion menu. ◎ *108 Bunda St, Civic • 6248 7109 • Open Mon–Sat • $$*

8 Lynwood Café
Just off the highway from Sydney to Canberra, this eatery offers hearty food to ease the long haul. Take home some jam. ◎ *1 Murray St, Collector • 4848 0200 • Open Thu–Sun • $*

9 Vulcan's
Join the Sydney foodies who head to Vulcan's to enjoy chef Phillip Searle's food. ◎ *33 Govetts Leap Rd, Blackheath • 4787 6899 • Open dinner and lunch Fri–Sun • $$*

10 Coffee Culture
It's a local secret that the best coffee in the Southern Highlands comes from this aromatic shop, hidden behind a cinema on Bowral's main street. ◎ *Shop 6, Empire Cinema Complex, 327 Bong Bong St, Bowral • 4862 2400 • $–$$*

Coffee Culture

Unless otherwise stated, all restaurants are open daily, accept credit cards, serve vegetarian meals, and provide disabled access.

STREETSMART

SYDNEY'S TOP 10

Left **Casual dress at a beachside café** Right **All non-Australians need passports**

Planning Your Trip

1 When to Go
Late spring (October–November) and early autumn (March-April) are the best times to visit Sydney. The days are warm and the evenings mild. Sydney's winters are cool to mild, but summer can be hot and unbearably humid with the occasional downpour.

2 What to Bring
Sydney fashion is casual, so a selection of light mix-and-match clothing should suffice. Be sure to pack beach gear and walking shoes.

3 How Long to Stay
One week will allow you to cover all the top 10 sights, in two weeks you'll be able to explore the Around Town section, and three weeks will be enough time to experience the national parks and outlying regions.

4 Media
Sydney has three major dailies. *The Sydney Morning Herald, The Daily Telegraph* and *The Australian,* all of which have websites. *The Sydney Morning Herald* is probably the best starting point to research events in Sydney.

5 Websites
The New South Wales (NSW) government portal is an informative site, and its Culture and Recreation section is useful for planning a holiday. The Australian Tourist Commission site provides information on various events and lists worldwide Australian travel agencies.

6 Passports & Visas
All foreign visitors to Australia must have a valid passport. If you are a New Zealander you will receive an electronic visa. If you are from any other country, you will require an entry visa or ETA (Electronic Travel Authority). Visa forms are available from travel agencies and the Australian government's immigration website.

7 Australian Consulates & Embassies
Australian consulates, embassies and missions are found in almost every country's capital city. They can provide information about Sydney and answer questions regarding visas. To locate the consulate in your city, visit the site listed under "Consulates".

8 Insurance
Although travel in Australia is generally straightforward, and hospitals won't turn you away if you're uninsured, it's always best to be insured when traveling. Before any challenging outdoor activity, read the fine print to ensure that you will be covered in emergency.

9 Driver's Licenses
Drivers with a valid overseas license in English can drive in Australia. Carry your license at all times if you are driving. Seatbelts are compulsory.

10 Customs
Customs regulations are strictly enforced and prohibit the unauthorised import of goods made from plant or animal products, weapons or firearms, protected wildlife, amounts exceeding $10,000 and non-prescription drugs. If you require medication, carry your prescription.

Directory

The Sydney Morning Herald
• www.smh.com.au

The Daily Telegraph
• www.dailytelegraph.news.com.au

The Australian
• www.theaustralian.news.com.au

NSW Government
• www.nsw.gov.au

Australian Tourist Commission
• www.australia.com

Australian Immigration
• www.immi.gov.au

Consulates
• www.embassy.gov.au

Customs
• www.customs.gov.au

Previous pages: **Monorail and Sydney Tower, City Centre**

Left **Flight arriving at the airport** Centre **Passenger train** Right **The QEII passenger ship**

🔟 Getting To Sydney

1 Kingsford-Smith International Airport

Sydney's only international airport is 9 km (5.6 miles) south of the city centre. Most domestic flights also arrive and depart from here. The international (T1) and domestic terminals (T2 and T3) are far apart, so you'll need to catch a taxi, bus or train to travel between them. Airport Link takes 2 minutes, but first check if your airline offers a free shuttle.

2 Airport Link

Trains provide a fast and easy way to get into the city, particularly at peak hour when traffic is heavy. The trip takes only 13 minutes. Use the elevators to get to the stations, directly below the terminals.

3 Airport Buses & Shuttles

Though very cheap, buses are only a good option if you are heading to Randwick, Coogee or Bondi Junction. Private shuttles such as Super-shuttle and Sydney Airporter are more expensive, but can be booked for specific times and will take you right to your destination.

4 Help Desks

Can't make up your mind where to go or what to do next? Visit the NSW Tourism Information Desks at the airport and at Central Station.

5 Taxis

A taxi (see p134) from T1 to the CBD costs about $30. There are ranks outside each terminal. A $2.50 toll has to be paid if you take a taxi from any of these. Taxi queues are longest on weekdays at 7–9am and 5–7pm, the airport's peak hours.

6 Car Hire

Car companies (see p134), have desks at the airport. Hiring a small car will cost $40–$80 per day, so it's advisable to shop around.

7 Central Station

All interstate and regional trains terminate on the upper level of this station. Many coach services drop passengers here, at the Sydney Coach Terminal. Suburban train services run from the lower level, buses to the eastern suburbs leave from Eddy Avenue, and those to the inner-west suburbs from nearby Railway Square. There is a taxi rank at the upper level entrance.

8 Passenger Ship Terminals

Both passenger ports, the Overseas Passenger Terminal (OPT) at West Circular Quay and Wharf 8 at Darling Harbour, are excellent places to arrive, centrally located and close to many hotels. The OPT is spectacular as it faces the Opera House.

9 Left Luggage

Due to new security policies, lockers are not available at the airport. Luggage can be left in the baggage storage areas of the arrivals hall in each terminal. There are no left luggage facilities at Central Station or at the ports.

🔟 Lost Property

Collect lost property from Sydney Airport Reception at T1. Contact your airline if your luggage goes missing or is left on the baggage carousel, or if you lose an item in T2 or T3. Items lost on a train or at a station can be found at Cityrail's lost property office at Central Station.

Directory

Airport Link
• *Runs every 10 mins on weekdays, every 15 mins on weekends*

Superbus
• 1000 765 606

Sydney Airporter
• 9666 9988

NSW Tourism Information Desks
• *Airport: T1 level 1; open 6am–11pm*
• *Central Station: main concourse, 6am–10pm*

Lost Property
• *Sydney Airport Reception: T1 level 3; 9667 9583* • *Cityrail: Central Station, main concourse; 9379 3341*

Left **The Sydney Explorer bus** Right **Circular Quay**

TOP 10 Getting Around

1 Buses
Bus services run frequently and are a good, cheap way to get around, although traffic can be very heavy at rush hour. Routes denoted with an "L," "E" or "X" indicate services that travel a greater distance between stops. Many buses leave from Circular Quay, so look out for the signs and maps.

2 Trains
Trains to most areas leave from the Town Hall and Central stations. Services run frequently from 6am until after midnight. There are heavy fines for smoking, littering or placing feet on seats.

3 Ferries
Sydney Ferries (see pp16–17) run services from Circular Quay to 41 wharves. The 30-minute ride from Circular Quay to Manly is extra special, but those who find it too long can catch the Jet Cat. Though not cheap, ferries are a great way to see Sydney and to experience the harbour.

4 Light Rail
A pleasant and fast way to get around, this is easily the best direct transport from the CBD to the Fish Market.

5 Monorail
Expensive but great fun, the monorail snakes through Sydney's CBD in a loop that takes in the Galeries Victoria, city centre, Darling Harbour, Powerhouse Museum, Chinatown and World Square. The trains depart every 5 minutes.

6 Taxis
Make bookings if you want to arrive at an exact time, especially at peak hours and on weekend nights. If drivers don't know the way, you are entitled to have them turn off the meter while they look up the street directory. Fares are regulated and cost more after 10pm. Smoking is not allowed and a driver may refuse to take you if you are drunk.

7 Water Taxis
Running from most piers, they'll pick you up from anywhere they can navigate. Prices vary, but expect to pay a flagfall of about $45 and an additional cost per person. Look for them at Circular Quay, or call to book one.

8 Explorer Buses
Great value tickets allow you to get on and off the buses at will, and frequent services run the loop. A two-day twin ticket allows you to travel on both Sydney and Bondi Explorers.

9 Car Hire
While the public transport network is excellent, having a car in Sydney makes getting around easy, particularly in the outer suburbs. A good street directory is essential, and you can use your usual license if you show proof that you're just visiting.

10 Bicycles
There are some cycle lanes on Sydney roads, making travel by bicycle safer and easier than ever before. Download a cycle map and hire a bike for a day or week from Cheeky Monkey or Woolys Wheels.

Directory

Light Rail
• *Runs 24 hours from Central to Star City*

Taxis
• *Taxis Combined: 133 300*
• *Legion Cabs: 131 451*

Water Taxis
• *9555 8888*

Explorer Buses
• *131 500; one-day ticket: $39; two-day twin ticket: $68*

Car Hire Companies
• *Hertz: 133039 • Bayswater 9360 3622 • Europcar: 1300 131 390*

Bicycle Information
• *Maps: www.rta.nsw. gov.au*
• *Cheeky Monkey: 28 Clovelly Rd; 9399 3370*
• *Woolys Wheels: 82 Oxford St; 9331 2671*

Transport Infoline
• *www.131500.com.au*
• *131500*

For discounted travel passes for regular buses, Explorer buses, ferries, airport train transfers and harbour cruises, see p140.

Left **Sydney Visitors Centre** Centre **Information kiosk at Central Station** Right **Children playing**

🔟 Sources of Information

1 Tourist Offices
The Sydney Visitors Centre at The Rocks *(see p140)* and Darling Harbour offer information and maps. You'll find City Host information kiosks at Circular Quay, Sydney Square and Martin Place. The Visitors Centre at Sydney Airport handles accommodation and travel bookings.

2 Embassies & Consulates
Several nations have consulates in Sydney, which can be located in the Yellow Pages telephone directory.

3 Disabled Travellers
Travellers with disabilities will find the Access Foundation's site an excellent resource for news, entertainment travel, accommodation, transport and links to community resources.

4 Gay & Lesbian Travellers
The Gay and Lesbian Tourism site provides accommodation information, while the *Sydney Star Observer* has news and entertainment listings. Gay Travel Guides publishes the *Sydney Gay and Lesbian Visitor's Guide. Lesbians on the Loose* has information, contacts and classifieds

5 Travelling with Children
Sydney's Child is a free monthly magazine with

tips for parents. Many venues also host kids programmes, so call ahead for information.

6 Older Travellers
The Senior Card and Seniors Information Service sites offer event listings, news and links to relevant organisations. *Get Up and Go* magazine contains information on travel agencies.

7 Websites
The City of Sydney and City Search websites cover sports, festivals, music, travel, exhibitions, tours, the arts and more.

8 Radio & TV
Five free TV stations include SBS and ABC. Triple J (105.7 FM) is an alternative music station, and 2SER FM (107.3) and FBI FM (94.5) are also worth checking out. 702 ABC (702 AM) serves up current affairs and drive-time formats while Radio National (576 AM) presents current affairs, music and culture.

9 Free Publications & Listings
City Weekly and *9 to 5* are weekly newspapers covering entertainment and leisure. The *Sydney Morning Herald*'s Metro section offers information on Sydney events.

10 Bookshops & Café Windows
Many independent bookshops and cafés

have noticeboards with local advertisements, especially around Glebe Point Road, Crown Street, King Street and Campbell Parade.

Directory

Sydney Visitor Centre
• 9240 8788 or freecall 1800 067 676

Consulates
• New Zealand: 8256 2000 • Canada: 9364 3000 • India: 9223 9635 • Ireland: 9264 6999 • UK: 9247 7521 • USA: 9373 9200

Yellow Pages
• www.yellowpages. com.au

Access Foundation
• www.accessibility. com.au

Sydney's Child
• www.sydneyschild. com.au

City Sites
• www.cityofsydney. nsw.gov.au • sydney. citysearch.com.au

Gay & Lesbian Sites
• www.galta.com.au
• www.ssonet.com.au
• www.gaytravelguides. com.au
• www.lotl.com

Seniors Sites
• www.seniorscard. nsw.gov.au
• www.getupandgo. net.au

Left **50-cent and $1 coins** Centre **$20 bill** Right **Phone card**

TOP 10 Banking & Communications

1 Money, Taxes & Refunds

The Australian dollar is divided into 100 cents. There are $5, $10, $20, $50 and $100 plastic notes. A 10 percent tax is levied on most goods and services (GST), but tourists may be entitled to refunds from Customs through the Tourist Refund Scheme (TRS). Be sure to ask for a "tax invoice" for purchases over $300, just in case.

2 Banks & Post Offices

Most banks are open from 9/10am–4/5pm Monday to Friday. Australia Post branch hours vary, but most are open from 9am–5pm Monday to Friday. The GPO is open from 8:15am–5:30pm Monday to Friday and 10am–2pm Saturday. Poste Restante mail should be addressed to the GPO, 1 Martin Place, Sydney 2000.

3 Public Holidays

Banks, post offices and most government agencies are closed on these public holidays: New Year's Day, Australia Day (26 January), Good Friday and Easter Monday, Anzac Day (25 April), Queen's Birthday (2nd Monday in June), Bank Holiday (1st Monday in August), Labour Day (1st Monday in October), Christmas Day and Boxing Day (26 December). The summer school

break extends from late December to late January. There are usually two-week breaks in April, July and September.

4 Currency Exchange

Bureaux de change at the airport open between 5am and 6am and close between 9:45pm and 11pm daily. There are numerous bureaux de change in the CBD.

5 Traveller's Cheques

Traveller's cheques are still accepted by major hotels, banks and the like, but personal cheques from foreign accounts are not.

6 ATMs

Most ATMs are located outside banks, and can also be found in many pubs and clubs. If your bank's debit card is linked to an international system such as Cirrus, you can use your card at retail outlets. Make sure that your PIN applies to Australian ATMs.

7 Credit Cards

MasterCard and Visa are the two major credit cards in Australia, although numerous establishments also accept American Express and Diners Club. Cash advances against your credit card are also possible. In most cases you'll need a credit card to hire a car in Sydney.

8 Telephones

Public telephones accept coins, phone cards and sometimes credit cards. A local call costs 40 cents. Phone cards are available at newsagents and convenience stores; make sure the card allows international calls before buying one. You can also rent a mobile phone for the duration of your stay.

9 Internet Access

Most hotels are set up to allow you to log on to the net. There is also no shortage of Internet cafés across the city.

10 Tipping

While tipping is not compulsory, it is always appreciated – 10 percent of the total bill is appropriate for good service. It is common to round up taxi fares, and hotel staff at exclusive establishments usually expect a gratuity.

Directory

Customs
• www.customs.gov.au

Stolen Credit Cards
• MasterCard: 1800 120 113 • Visa: 1800 450 346 • Amex: 1300 132 639 • Diners Club: 1300 360 060

Mobile Phone Rental
• Vodafone Rentals: Sydney Airport: 1800 144 340

The International prefix to dial Australia is 61. The area code for Sydney is 02. Numbers preceded by 04 are mobile numbers.

Left **Police vehicle** Centre **Pharmacy in The Rocks** Right **Lifesaving sign**

Security & Health

1 Theft
Sydney is a safe destination, but the usual "Big City" rules apply. Don't leave valuables in cars, avoid ATMs late at night, and be alert to pickpockets at train stations. Baggage storage is available at the airport, and lockers at the State Library, most swimming pools and at Bondi and Manly.

2 Dangerous Areas
Avoid parks, barren areas and the back-streets of Kings Cross late at night. If you're travelling on a train alone at night, sit near the guard's compartment.

3 Hospitals & Medical Centres
Sydney Hospital, St Vincent's Hospital and the Sydney Children's Hospital are the most central facilities that accept emergency admissions. If you require an ambulance, dial 000. Make sure your travel insurance covers ambulance fees, which can be expensive.

4 Pharmacies
Pharmacies are found all over Sydney. In some suburbs they open on weekends according to a roster. If one is closed, there is usually a sign indicating the nearest open pharmacy. It's advisable to carry your prescription if you require regular medication.

5 Women Travellers
Sydney can be "blokey" (macho), but women travellers mostly find it a relaxed and casual city. The WIRS (Women's Information and Referral Service) has information on women's services and organisations. The Rape Crisis Centre can also help in an emergency.

6 Things that Bite & Sting
Sydneysiders are obsessed with creatures that bite and sting, such as sharks and blue-ringed octopus, but you'd be unlikely to encounter them. Blowflies and "mozzies" can be annoying in summer, but they don't carry malaria. Do wear sturdy shoes and long trousers if walking in bushland.

7 Ticks & Other Nasties
Bush ticks are small insects that drop from foliage and burrow into your skin; check your scalp if you've been bushwalking. Sodium bicarbonate helps to remove ticks. For further information visit www.tickalert.org.au

8 Sunburn
Take precautions against the strong Australian sun, for even overcast days can have a high UV rating. Keep in mind that water amplifies the intensity of UV rays.

9 Swimming
Unless you are an experienced open-water swimmer, stick to beaches patrolled by lifeguards. If caught in an undertow (see p138), don't try swimming against the current; wait until help arrives or the rip peters out.

10 Bushfires
Bushfires are part of Sydney life, especially in the bushy outer suburbs. "Total Fire Ban" days are often declared in summer. If you're in trouble, don't try to outrun the fire: seek shelter immediately to avoid the most common cause of death in this situation, which is radiant heat.

Directory

Hospitals & Clinics
• Sydney Hospital: 8 Macquarie St
• St. Vincent's Hospital: Victoria St, Darlinghurst
• Sydney Children's Hospital: High St, Randwick

Women's Resources
• WIRS: 1800 817 227 www.women.nsw.gov. au • Rape Crisis Centre: 24 hrs daily; 9819 7357; freecall 1800 424 017

Emergencies
• Fire, Police, Ambulance: freecall 000
• Lifeline: 131 114
• Poisons Information Line: 131 126

137

Left **Lifesaving flag** Right **Central Railway Station**

Things to Avoid

1 Swimming Outside the Flags

Although Sydney beaches are idyllic, their unpredictable rips (undertows) can be hazardous. Always swim between the flags and ensure that you are being watched by a lifeguard. If you get into trouble, try to relax and raise an arm to alert the lifeguards.

2 Upturning an Empty Schooner

If you wander into one of Sydney's pubs and the bloke next to you places his empty "schooner" upside down on the beer-soaked counter, make a beeline for the exit. This is shorthand for "I'll take on all comers". And don't ever try it yourself.

3 Age Restrictions

Age restrictions apply to entry to licensed premises and gambling venues, 18 years in both instances. Cigarettes are not sold to under 18-year olds and there are stiff penalties if caught buying for minors. There are also heavy penalties if caught with illicit drugs.

4 Walking into Traffic

If you're fresh off the plane from Los Angeles or New York and feeling a little jetlagged, look both ways before stepping off the pavement (sidewalk): Australian cars drive on the left-hand side of the road, not the right.

5 Beggars & the Homeless

Like any big city, Sydney has its share of homeless beggars, most of whom present no danger. Some of them are registered street vendors of *The Big Issue*; purchase a copy if you'd like to support those trying to get back on their feet. They get half the proceeds and it's a good read.

6 Drink Driving

Drink driving is a problem in Australia and police are equipped to test drivers for alcohol. The legal limit is 0.05. "Booze buses" (police teams with testing equipment) randomly target major roads at odd hours. If caught, your car keys will be confiscated and you will face a hefty fine. It's just not worth the risk, so catch a taxi.

7 City Circle Train Stations at Peak Hour

Sydney's central underground railway stations are frantic at peak hour. Not just busy, they can be stiflingly hot, especially in summer. Like all congested city venues they are frequented by pickpockets, so be careful.

8 Praising Melbourne

There is a long and robust history of rivalry between Sydney and Melbourne. If you visited Melbourne and were impressed by the southern city's Victorian charms, don't go on about them to the first Sydneysider you meet. Sydney's residents are firmly convinced they are living in God's Own City, and nothing will annoy them more.

9 You say Bond-ee, I say Bond-eye

North Americans are prone to stumbling into this minefield. Bondi is pronounced "Bond-eye", not "Bond-ee". For some reason Sydneysiders find this mistake particularly irksome. Some other pronunciation pitfalls include "Mel-born" instead of "Mel-bun" for Melbourne, and "Coo-gee" instead of "Could-gee" for Coogee Beach. French speakers will probably be horrified at the Australian pronunciation of the southern suburb of Sans Souci.

10 Bluebottles

Strong winds can bring bluebottles onto beaches: they look like blue jellyfish and have long stinging tentacles. Their sting is painful but they are only dangerous for people with asthma. Dead bluebottles stranded on the sand can still sting. Avoid swimming near them, don't rub a sting and if no medical attention is available, treat with ice packs.

Peak hours run between 7–9am and 5–7pm on weekdays.

Left **Paddington Market** Centre **Darling Harbour** Right **The Strand**

Shopping Tips

1 Trading Hours
Most stores are open daily 9am–5:30pm, with some closing early on Sundays. Late-night shopping on Thursdays sees shops open until 9pm. In areas such as Paddington, Balmain and Double Bay, shops open between 10 and 11am and close at 6pm. Many shops in Chinatown are open until 7pm daily.

2 Sales
While boutiques no longer stick to a firm schedule of sales, department stores have huge sales in December and again in June. There are great bargains, especially on homewares. Sales are usually advertised in *The Sydney Morning Herald (see p132)*.

3 GST
A Goods and Services Tax (GST) of ten percent is applied to most items. If you spend more than $300 at any one shop within 28 days of leaving Australia, you are entitled to re claim the GST. Take your receipts to the booth at Sydney Airport.

4 Payment
All stores accept credit cards, though some claim a surcharge on credit card purchases. Some larger stores, souvenir shops and duty free stores may accept traveller's cheques with passport identification.

5 Warehouse Outlets
Many local chain stores and manufacturers have warehouse outlets in inner city suburbs such as Alexandria. The best way to check them out is on a day tour. Try Sydney Shopping tours, which has six city pick-up points and includes lunch.

6 Souvenirs
For stuffed koalas, you can't beat the discount shops on Pitt and Park Streets. Most attractions offer quality keepsakes; try the Museum of Sydney *(see p42)* and Opera House Store *(see p81)*. Buy opals and boomerangs in The Rocks *(see p81)*, swimwear and T-shirts at surf shops *(see p94)* and sheepskins in the QVB *(see p80)*. Try the week end market at The Rocks for handmade items.

7 Fashion & Accessories
You'll find high-end designer fashion in Double Bay and in the WBJ luxury mall *(see p100)*. A younger crowd shops in the Galeries Victoria *(see p80)*, Paddington *(see p94)* and Woollahra for casual and party clothes. Try Newtown *(see p106)* for alternative and second-hand shops, including goth shops lining Enmore Road. Find kids' clothes at David Jones *(see p81)* and WBJ.

8 Design & Homewares
The best of Australian and international design can be found in Surry Hills and Alexandria. A stroll around the streets near Central station will unearth gems. Crown Street between Foveaux and Devonshire is also a great strip *(see p94)*. The Object store *(see p44)* has a great range of Australian design crafts.

9 Food
The big supermarkets are mostly found in the suburbs, but there is a Woolworths at Town Hall station and a Coles at Wynyard. Delicatessens offer great sandwich fillings, small goods and cheese. David Jones' food hall offers gourmet goodies as well as pre-cooked dinners. Grower's markets, advertised in *The Sydney Morning Herald* on Tuesdays, are a wonderful way to shop.

10 Going Green
A current campaign to reduce the quantity of plastic bags that end up as landfill has caused shops to introduce many eco-friendly options. Buy a sturdy, reusable green bag – fast becoming trendy – from Coles or Woolworths supermarkets, department stores and even smaller shops, or pack your purchases into your backpack.

Contact Sydney Shopping Tours at 1800 673 709 or www.sydneyshoppingtours.com.au – a day's tour costs $50.

Streetsmart

Left **TravelPasses** Centre **Picnic basket** Right **Laundromat**

🔟 Sydney on a Budget

1 Discount Plane Tickets
There are often cheap tickets to Australia available in the low season, from mid-April to end-September. If flying in from elsewhere in Australia, check out the websites of discount air carriers Virgin and Jetstar for good deals.

2 Hotel Deals
Look for packages that offer free or very cheap accommodation when you buy your flights. You can also find cheap rates by booking hotels online, or by making week-long reservations *(see p142)*.

3 Youth Hostels
Staying in hostels is not just for backpackers, as most have comfortable double and twin rooms available for modest prices. You'll also benefit from the use of the kitchen, fridge, laundry and lounge areas. Many hostels have swimming pools.

4 Concessions
An International Student Identification Card, available from STA travel agents, will get you a concession entry into most attractions, galleries and museums, but not the concession rate on public transport.

5 TravelPasses
Weekly passes for unlimited trips on buses, trains and ferries can save plenty of money. A green TravelPass should take you anywhere you want to go. It is great value, particularly if you're planning on making more than two trips a day. TravelTens, which don't expire and can be shared, also save money; buy a blue ten-trip bus pass and dip it twice if you're going further than two zones. However, these passes cannot be used on the monorail and light rail services.

6 Phone Cards
Convenience stores all over the city sell international calling cards, so shop around for one with good rates. Buy a Telstra phone card to use for local calls.

7 Cheap Eats
Sydney has myriad cheap and cheerful restaurants. The best are often small local diners offering Thai, Chinese, Indian or Lebanese food. To save more money, bring your own wine or beer and stop by a gelataria for an ice cream or gelato dessert.

8 Coupons
There are often vouchers for Sydney's top restaurants among the brochures in high-end hotel lobbies. Stop by one of these hotels and rummage through the racks; you may find offers such as two main courses for the price of one. More coupons may be available at the Sydney Visitors' Centre.

9 Picnics
Buying lunch every day can be expensive. Instead, buy staples such as bread, fruit and cheese and store them in the fridge at your hostel or hotel room. Make a picnic lunch and pack it for the day. Sydney's tap water is good quality, so buy a bottle of water and keep refilling it.

10 Laundromats
Hostels usually have coin-operated washing machines, but if you're staying somewhere without one, avoid the cost of laundering by going to a laundromat. If you don't want to stick around, opt for a bag wash, which costs about $6. Otherwise, use the coin-operated machines.

Directory

STA Travel
841 George St, Sydney; 9212 1255

Sydney Visitors' Centre
• Cnr Argyle & Playfair Sts, The Rocks; 9240 8788

Laundromats
Laundrette on King: 409 King St, Newtown • Soap Sud City: 56 Bayswater Rd, Kings Cross

Left **Wine bottle label** Centre **Fresh produce** Right **Making coffee at Bar Colluzi**

10 Dining Tips

1 Mod Oz
Modern Australian cuisine is generally a fusion of Asian and Eastern flavours with European technique. Experimental Australian chefs draw on the highly multicultural population and a diverse climate that ranges from tropical to cool-region conditions.

2 Menu Jargon
The quest for the exotic generates menus loaded with foreign terms and regional Australian names. Bangalow and Barossa refer to regions; Wagyu and Hiramasa to quality, assiétte, confit and panacotta to French and Italian techniques. Menus are sometimes in a different language, and Chinese restaurants often have an English and a Chinese menu. Staff are usually happy to translate.

3 Courses
Pre-dinner nibbles are called hors d'oeuvres or canapés. The first course is the entrée, and the second is the main course. These are followed by dessert and coffee, or sometimes by a cheese course.

4 Dégustation
This French word means to take a small amount into the mouth and test its quality. A Sydney trend, dégustations offer 7–12 small set courses instead of orders from the menu. These courses allow chefs to take advantage of the freshest ingredients and to show off their skills.

5 Bookings
The more expensive the restaurant, the further ahead you'll need to make your reservation. Sydney's top restaurant, the dégustation-only Tetsuya's *(see p58)*, takes bookings three months in advance. Vegetarians and those with special dietary requirements should book at least a day ahead. Some restaurants don't take bookings but will send you to a nearby pub and call you when your table is ready.

6 Tipping
Usual but voluntary, tipping is a way to express your enjoyment of or dissatisfaction with a meal. If the food and service are of good quality, leave about 15 percent. You may want to leave more for extraordinary service, and less or no tip if service has been shoddy.

7 Wine
Most expensive restaurants have helpful sommeliers who are experts at matching food and wine, so you can leave the choices up to them. You might tell them that you wish to taste a variety of Australian wines. When buying wine from a bottle shop, be aware that Australian names refer to the grape variety and not the region.

8 Beer
Some types of food are highly spiced and do not go well with most wines. Choosing a beer to go with Thai, Indian and Chinese food is a good option. Good Australian beers include Boag's, Cascade, Hahn Premium, James Squire, Cooper's and Redback.

9 Coffee
The ubiquitous espresso coffee comes in various forms. A flat white is a shot of coffee with milk but no froth while the popular latte has additional milk and is served in a long glass. Try a macchiato, a shot topped with a burst of froth. Decaf, soy and light milks are common.

10 Dining With Children
Some restaurants specifically cater to kids with dedicated menus. Others will suggest entrée-sized dishes that might appeal to children. The large Chinese and Italian restaurants and places by the beach are usually used to kids running around. Bring some pens with you, as restaurants often have paper clothes or napkins that kids can draw on.

Some restaurants which are not licensed have a policy of BYO, or "bring your own" alcohol; at some others, BYO is optional.

Left **Hotels at Darling Harbour** Right **Comfortable hotel room**

Accommodation Tips

1 Choosing Hotel Locations
Staying at the beach means a refreshing dip is only moments away. Hotels on the fringe of the CBD, especially those with harbour views, are a relaxing option for business travellers. Those with children might avoid areas around Potts Point and Darlinghurst, which necessitate walking through the red light district of Kings Cross.

2 Making Reservations
It is advisable to make reservations. Book well in advance when Sydney is busiest, from mid-December until the beginning of February, during Mardi Gras in early March, and in the the first two weeks of April, July and October. Reservations can be made by contacting the hotel directly or through your travel agent.

3 Discount Rates
Some hotels offer significant discounts for last minute bookings and walk-ins. Hotel websites sometimes offer great rates. If you are prepared to make a non-refundable booking, you might get as much as a 50 percent discount on rooms.

4 Longer Stays
Some hotels, particularly hostels, budget and boutique hotels, reward guests for lengthy stays with reduced weekly rates. Many hostels set a limit of a 14-day stay. Serviced apartments may offer incentives for stays of up to a month.

5 Frequent Flyers
Most airline frequent flyer programmes have lists of hotels where members can accrue points. Existing points can usually be used for room upgrades or special packages. Airline bookings sometimes offer a discount.

6 Water Views
While many hotels are situated at the water's edge, the standard room rate usually applies to a room without a view. Expect to pay a premium of about $50–$100 above the standard rate. You might find better value in the best room of a smaller or lower-rated hotel.

7 Extra Costs
Even the most basic breakfast can be expensive in the large CBD hotels, so head to a nearby café or bakery. Drinks and snacks provided in the minibar are often double their retail cost, so check the prices first. Avoid surcharges on phone calls by using a public phone in the lobby. Other services, such as late checkouts, parking, laundering, Internet access, in-house movies and receiving faxes usually incur a fee.

8 Travelling with Children
Children under 12 usually stay for free using existing bedding. This can be a good arrangement in twin rooms that offer a double and single bed, or in studios that include sofa beds. Where offered, there is a fee of approximately $30 for rollaway beds. Many hotels can arrange interconnecting rooms.

9 Disabled Travellers
Regulations force larger hotels to offer rooms with full disabled access, and some hotels have as many as ten such rooms. The same rules don't apply to small hotels and B&Bs in converted mansions or heritage buildings. It's best to enquire about facilities when making reservations and to check that there is room to manoeuvre a wheelchair.

10 GST
GST *(see p139)* is charged on hotel rooms and on other services that hotels may provide for you. The tax is usually included in the room rate and will be clearly marked on any accounts. It is not possible to reclaim GST incurred on accommodation.

Price Categories

For a standard double room per night (with breakfast if included), taxes and extra charges.

$	under $80
$$	$80–150
$$$	$150–250
$$$$	$250–350
$$$$$	over $350

Exterior of Park Hyatt Sydney

🔟 Harbourside Hotels

1 Blue Sydney

This modern boutique hotel is one of the coolest in Sydney. Sip fabulous cocktails at the award-winning Water Bar and enjoy the luxury robes and Aveda bath products. ⊗ *Map P3 • The Wharf at Woolloomooloo, Cowper Wharf Rd • 9331 9000 • $$$$$ • www.tajhotels. com/sydney*

2 The Sebel Pier One Sydney

In a restored wharf building in the Walsh Bay World Heritage precinct, look right into the water through the lobby's glass floor. Luxurious rooms incorporate original features and contemporary design. ⊗ *Map M1 • 11 Hickson Rd, Walsh Bay • 8298 9999 • $$$$ • www.mirvachotels.com*

3 Vibe Hotel Rushcutters

Between the CBD and Bondi, this stylish hotel neighbours a harbourside park and overlooks the Cruising Yacht Club marina. A brisk walk up the hill takes you to Kings Cross and Darlinghurst. ⊗ *Map Q5 • 100 Bayswater Rd, Rushcutters Bay • 8353 8988 • $$$$ • www. vibehotels.com.au*

4 Park Hyatt Sydney

Many rooms in this luxurious six-star hotel have Opera House views, as does the rooftop heated swimming pool. Perfectly equipped for business travellers, the hotel offers high-speed Internet access in every room and a dedicated business centre. ⊗ *Map M1 • 7 Hickson Rd, The Rocks • 9241 1234 • $$$$$ • www.sydney. park.hyatt.com*

5 Four Seasons Hotel Sydney

You'll be able to spot this superbly-located high-rise hotel from many vantages. Inside, the higher the floor number, the better the view. Corner rooms have a full harbour panorama. The marble-clad lobby leads to lovely lounge areas and two fine restaurants. ⊗ *Map M2 • 199 George St, The Rocks • 9230 0000 • $$$$ • www. fourseasons.com/sydney*

6 Quay Grand Suites

Next door to the Opera House at one of Sydney's premier addresses, apartments are tastefully furnished with kitchen facilities. Try ECQ, the hotel's dress circle bar. ⊗ *Map N1 • 61 Macquarie St, East Circular Quay • 9256 4000 • Some dis access • $$$$ • www. mirvachotels.com*

7 Star City

You might think the casino tacky, but the hotel is first rate, with stylish rooms and an endless list of facilities. Drawcards include king beds in the standard rooms, 19 restaurants and bars, 24-hour entertainment and a health club with a pool. Choose between hotel and apartment-style accommodation. ⊗ *Map K3 • 80 Pyrmont St, Pyrmont • 1800 700 700 • $$$–$$$$$ • www.starcity.com.au*

8 Novotel Darling Harbour

Enjoy the benefits of staying in a very large hotel by choosing one of many different room configurations. This hotel is at the top end of the four-star range. ⊗ *Map L4 • 100 Murray St, Pyrmont • 9934 0000 • $$$–$$$$$ • www.novotel.com.au*

9 Ibis Darling Harbour

The pleasant three-star Ibis hotel is close to all the Darling Harbour attractions, and is a good alternative for a water view without the usual hefty charge. ⊗ *Map L4 • 70 Murray St, Darling Harbour • 0563 0000 • $$–$$$$ • www. ibishotels.com.au*

10 Holiday Inn Darling Harbour

The location's great and so is the Heritage-listed woolstore that houses the newly refurbished hotel. They offer good facilities for business travellers in the executive suites. ⊗ *Map L5 • 68 Harbour St, Darling Harbour • 9291 0200 • $$$ • www.holidayinn darlingharbour.com.au*

Unless otherwise stated, all hotels accept credit cards, have en-suite bathrooms and air conditioning and provide dis access.

143

Left **Dive** Right **Sebel Manly Beach**

🔟 Beachside Accommodation

1 Swiss-Grand Resort & Spa
This luxurious all-suite hotel has an unbeatable location at Bondi. It has full resort and day spa facilities, a rooftop swimming pool, and four bars and restaurants. ◈ Map H5 • Cnr Campbell Parade & Beach Rd, Bondi Beach • 9365 5666 • $$$$$ • www.swissgrand.com.au

2 Ravesi's
This lovely boutique hotel has recently been refurbished. Split-level suites cost more but are gorgeous, opening onto private terraces with ocean views. There is also a popular bar and a restaurant downstairs. ◈ Map H5 • 118 Campbell Parade, Bondi Beach • 9365 4422 • $$$–$$$$$ • www.ravesis.com.au

3 Dive
A stylish hotel featured in design magazines, its rooms have high ceilings and designer bathrooms. Complimentary breakfast and unlimited tea and coffee are available. The two front rooms have spectacular views. ◈ Map U4 • 234 Arden St, Coogee • 9665 5538 • No dis access • Some air conditioning • $$$ • www.divehotel.com.au

4 Coogee Bay Hotel
The raucous pub (see p97) is a beacon for backpackers, who can't resist the beachfront beer garden. While the heritage rooms above the pub are noisy, the adjoining boutique hotel is peaceful and comfortable. Rooms are excellent value, particularly those with ocean views. ◈ Map U4 • Cnr Coogee Bay Rd & Arden St, Coogee • 9315 6055 • $$$–$$$$ • www.coogeebayhotel.com.au

5 Sebel Manly Beach
Choose a lovely ocean view room or suite at this four-star hotel. The Sebel is close to Fairy Bower Beach and a delightful coastal walk (see p118). ◈ Map U3 • 8–13 South Steyne St, Manly • 9977 8866 • $$$$ • www.mirvac.com.au

6 Periwinkle Guesthouse
A striking Federation-era mansion has been converted into a B&B with antique furniture and tasteful colour schemes. Rooms with a view attract only a small premium. ◈ Map U3 • 18–19 East Esplanade, Manly • 9977 4668 • No dis access • No air conditioning • $$–$$$ • www.periwinkle.citysearch.com.au

7 Rydges Cronulla Beach
Most rooms in this great value hotel have views of the ocean. A great place to use as a base when exploring the Royal National Park, Cronulla is also packed with groovy restaurants and bars. ◈ Map T6 • 20–26 The Kingsway, Cronulla • 9527 3100 • $$$–$$$$ • www.rydges.com

8 Quest Cronulla
This apartment-style hotel offers fabulous ocean views. Rooms have Internet connections, fully equipped kitchens and laundries, and the hotel can arrange to stock up your pantry or to have dinner at a local restaurant charged to your room. ◈ Map T6 • 1 The Kingsway, Cronulla, • 8536 3600 • $$$ • www.questcronullabeach.com.au

9 Sydney Beachouse YHA
At this hostel on the northern beaches, spend days lounging by the pool, surfing, cycling or playing beach volleyball. There is a cinema next door, and Manly is only a bus ride away. ◈ Map U2 • 4 Collaroy St, Collaroy • 9981 1177 • Some air conditioning • $–$$ • www.sydneybeachouse.com.au

10 Jonah's
Have dinner at Jonah's and stay at their wonderful guesthouse. Each of the ten deluxe rooms has a private balcony with ocean views, a king bed and Jacuzzi. ◈ Map U1 • 69 Bynya Road, Palm Beach • 9974 5599 • $$$$$ • www.jonahs.com.au

Unless otherwise stated, all hotels accept credit cards, have en-suite bathrooms and air conditioning and provide dis access.

Left **Sofitel Wentworth Sydney** Right **The Westin Sydney**

TOP 10 Traditional Hotels

1 InterContinental Sydney

A beautiful 1851 Treasury building offers five-star luxury. The soaring foyer has a lovely lounge. All rooms have window seats, a chaise longue and views of the city or harbour and Botanic Gardens. ⊗ Map N2 • 117 Macquarie St • 9253 9000 • $$$$–$$$$$ • www. sydney.intercontinental.com

2 The Westin Sydney

In this glorious heritage building, rooms in the restored main building feature antique fittings, although the majority of rooms are in the new tower section. Find great restaurants and a food store in the GPO.
⊗ Map M3 • 1 Martin Place • 8223 1111 • $$$$ $$$$$ • www.westin.com.au

3 Stamford Plaza

Live old-world style at this sumptuous hotel. The lounge and dining areas are magnificent, the rooms are large and traditionally decorated, and the hotel's proximity to the classiest shopping precinct in Sydney is unbeatable. ⊗ Map F4 • 33 Cross St, Double Bay • 9362 4455 • $$$ • www. stamford.com.au

4 The Observatory Hotel

Book a package at the renowned day spa when you stay at this absolute luxury hotel. The hotel

caters especially well to business travellers, and runs one-way transfers into the central business district daily from 7–10am. ⊗ Map L2 • 89–113 Kent St • 9256 2222 • $$$$$ • www. observatoryhotel.com.au

5 Sheraton on the Park

Enjoy all the facilities you'd expect at a fine hotel, such as marble bathrooms, stylish furnishings, data ports, 24-hour room service, helpful concierges, baby-sitting services and lounges. ⊗ Map M5 • 161 Elizabeth St • 9286 6000 • $$$$$ • www.sheraton. com/sydney

6 Sofitel Wentworth Sydney

This building is a Sydney classic thanks to its curved, copper-clad façade. Inside, modern chandeliers feature hundreds of glass tear-drops, and throughout the hotel pale wood and rich, dark fabrics are used to maximum effect. ⊗ Map N3 • 61–101 Phillip St • 9230 0700 • $$$$–$$$$$ • www.sofitelsydney.com.au

7 Hilton

Re-opened in 2005 after massive renovations, the Hilton Sydney is one of the city's premier landmarks. Alongside super chef Luke Mangan's glass brasserie and New York designer Tony Chi's Zeta bar, the luxurious guest rooms include

relaxation suites. ⊗ Map M4 • 488 George St • 9266 2000 • $$$$$ • www.hiltonsydney.com.au

8 Castlereagh Boutique Hotel

Full of character, this well-located hotel is great value. The rooms here, full of period furniture and patterned upholstery, offer essentials such as TVs, bars, fridges and tea and coffee facilities. ⊗ Map M4 • 169 Castlereagh St • 9284 1000 • Limited dis access • $$$–$$$$ • www. thecastlereagh.net.au

9 The Grace Hotel

You couldn't be closer to the action than at The Grace. The restored hotel dates from the 1930s and its refurbishment has retained the building's original Art Deco style. ⊗ Map M3 • 77 York St • 9272 6888 • $$$–$$$$$ • www.gracehotel.com.au

10 The Russell

A lovely old-fashioned hotel sits above a historic pub, the Fortune of War. The Russell offers complimentary breakfast, a quaint guest sitting room, well-stocked library and sunny rooftop garden overlooking the busy Rocks area. Some rooms have shared bathrooms. ⊗ Map M2 • 143a George St, The Rocks • 9241 3543, • No dis access • Some air conditioning • $$ $$$ • www.therussell.com.au

Room rates may vary with season, availability, specials and promotions. All prices listed are high-season rates.

Left **Medusa's courtyard** Centre **Establishment** Right **Kirketon**

TOP 10 Boutique Hotels

1 Kirketon
This boutique hotel is an oasis of style, glamour and comfort in the heart of the vibrant suburb of Darlinghurst. The Kirketon Dining Room and Bar offers a contemporary dining experience inspired by the iconic brasseries of Paris. ◎ Map P5 • 229 Darlinghurst Rd, Darlinghurst • 9332 2011 • No dis access • $$$ • www.kirketon.com.au

2 Medusa
Medusa makes its own rules as only a boutique hotel can, and traditional room fittings have been replaced by a strong modernist look. Lindt chocolates and Aveda toiletries are complimentary, as is use of a neighbouring gym. There's also a business room available and dogs are allowed in some rooms. ◎ Map P5 • 267 Darlinghurst Rd, Darlinghurst • 9331 1000 • No dis access • $$$$$ • www.medusa.com.au

3 Establishment
This is one of the most fashionable and desirable places in town. Two suites and 33 rooms offer a choice of lively or tranquil colour schemes, marble or stone bathrooms with separate baths and showers, thick sheets, and CD and DVD players. ◎ Map M2 • 5 Bridge Lane • 9240 3100 • $$$$–$$$$$ • www. establishmenthotel.com

4 L'Otel
A large terrace house has been converted into a stylish hotel with small but lovely rooms. There's a hip bar and restaurant downstairs, and the hotel is close to Oxford Street's cafés and bars. ◎ Map P5 • 114 Darlinghurst Rd, Darlinghurst • 9360 6868 • No dis access • $$$–$$$$ • www.lotel.com.au

5 Blacket
A former 1850s bank, the hotel has retained its original features. Various configurations of rooms are available, all stylishly furnished. Ask about deals that include dinner at the Level Three restaurant, where you can also have breakfast. ◎ Map M3 • 70 King St • 9279 3030 • $$$–$$$$ • www.theblacket.com

6 Central Park
Their "hip on a budget" slogan is a great description of this hotel. Its reasonably-priced studio rooms and light and airy New York-style loft suites are complemented by neutral colours and clean-lined furniture. ◎ Map M4 • 185 Castlereagh St • 9283 5000 • No dis access • $$$ • www.centralpark.com.au

7 Vulcan Hotel
A high-class hotel for businessmen when it opened in 1894, the Vulcan had a stint as a student jazz bar until it was refurbished. The minimal rooms are fabulous value. Breakfast at Hummingbird restaurant is great. ◎ Map L6 • 500 Wattle St, Ultimo • 9211 3283 • $$ • www. vulcanhotel.com.au

8 Lord Nelson
Get a taste of Colonial Sydney in the pretty rooms at this famous sandstone pub. The accommodation includes modern necessities such as dataports. Breakfast is included. ◎ Map L1 • 19 Kent St • 9251 4044 • No dis access • $$ • www.lordnelson.com.au

9 Altamont
At this fun budget hotel, all rooms have cable TV and solid, comfy wooden furniture. There are discount weekly rates and a few top-quality backpacker rooms: they fill up quickly, so book them early. ◎ Map P5 • 207 Darlinghurst Road, Darlinghurst • 9360 6000 • No dis access • $$ • www.altamont.com.au

10 Tricketts B&B
At this grand old gentleman's residence, large bedrooms are lovingly restored. The house is furnished with antiques and Persian carpets. ◎ Map C4 • 270 Glebe Point Rd, Glebe • 9552 1141 • No dis access • $$$ • www.tricketts.com.au

Unless otherwise stated, all hotels accept credit cards, have en-suite bathrooms and air conditioning and provide dis access.

Price Categories

For a standard double room per night (with breakfast if included), taxes and extra charges.

$	under $80
$$	$80–150
$$$	$150–250
$$$$	$250–350
$$$$$	over $350

The Chelsea

⁑10 Gay & Lesbian Friendly Hotels

1 The Chelsea
At this beautiful guesthouse, decorated in French Provincial and contemporary styles, your stay is made tranquil by attentive hosts and a quiet street. ⬭ Map Q5 • 49 Womerah Ave, Darlinghurst • 9380 5994 • No dis access • $$–$$$ • www.chelsea guesthouse.com.au

2 Hughenden
This former gentleman's mansion is a Woollahra institution. Writers' groups meet and artists exhibit their work within its walls, providing a connection to the surrounding arty community. ⬭ Map E5 • 14 Queen St, Woollahra • 9363 4863 • No dis access • $$$$ • www.hughendenhotel. com.au

3 Simpsons
A charming B&B at the "Paris" end of Potts Point, where the complimentary breakfast is served in a glass roofed conservatory. Guests staying in the romantic Cloud Suite enjoy chocolates, flowers and champagne when booked under the Honeymoon Package. ⬭ Map P3 • 8 Challis Ave • 9356 2199 • No dis access • $$$–$$$$ • www.simpsonshotel.com

4 Sullivans
Standard rooms at this friendly hotel face the bustle of Oxford Street. It's worth paying a tiny bit more for a garden room which overlooks the courtyard and swimming pool. Guests can use the Internet, pool, gym, in-house movies and bicycles. ⬭ Map P6 • 21 Oxford St, Paddington • 9361 0211 • $$–$$$ • www.sullivans.com.au

5 Azure Executive Apartments
Though not particularly stylish, these apartments are clean and spacious. Great for a long stay, they offer dining areas and kitchenettes. Most have balconies and good views. ⬭ Map Q3 • 40 Macleay St, Potts Point • 9356 6900 • No dis access • $$$ • www. azureapartments.com

6 Quality Hotel Cambridge
This well-located hotel is close to many gay bars and clubs. Rooms are great value and amenities include 24-hour room service, a heated pool, gym, spa and sauna. ⬭ Map N6 • 212 Riley St, Surry Hills • 9212 1111 • $$ • www.cambridgesydney hotel.com.au

7 Victoria Court
Historic 1881 buildings have been transformed into a delightful B&B. Most rooms have marble fireplaces, some have four poster beds and all are decked out in authentic period furniture. In winter, snuggle up by the fire in the guest lounge. ⬭ Map P4 • 122 Victoria St, Potts Point • 9357 3200 • No dis access • $$–$$$ • www.victoriacourt.com.au

8 BIG Hostel
A new hostel offers dorm rooms, doubles and triples, and is a great place to meet people. BIG has great facilities, including a slick kitchen, lounge area, projector screen and complimentary breakfast. ⬭ Map M5 • 212 Elizabeth St, Surry Hills • 9281 6030 • $$ • www.bighostel.com

9 Rydges Camperdown
One of the few hotels in the gay and lesbian enclaves of Camperdown. The hotel is also near Parramatta Road, where buses leave for the city and Leichhardt. Relax in the pool or sauna. ⬭ Map B5 • 9 Missenden Rd, Camperdown • 9516 1522 • $$–$$$ • www. rydges.com/camperdown

10 Macleay Apartments
There are excellent value weekly rates available at this hotel. The clean apartments have well-equipped kitchenettes and are a great choice for busy travellers. There's a rooftop pool and barbecue area. ⬭ Map Q3 • 28 Macleay St, Potts Point • 9357 7755 • Limited dis access • $$$ • www.themacleay.com

Room rates may vary with season, availability, specials and promotions. All prices listed are high-season rates.

147

Left **Apartment at Stellar Suites** Right **Manly Bungalow**

🔟 Budget Hotels & Hostels

1 Y Hotel
Expect less of the party crowd at this peaceful backpacker spot since all dorm rooms have just four single beds and are single-sex. There's coffee, tea and breakfast included in the room price. Standard double rooms are basic but clean. ⓢ *Map N5 • 5–11 Wentworth Ave • 9264 2451 • Dis access • Air conditioning • $–$$ • www.yhotel.com.au*

2 Railway Square YHA
Old railway buildings house this new super-hostel. The entrance is via a platform and some rooms are inside railway carriages. Its facilities include a 24-hour reception and spa pool. ⓢ *Map M6 • 8–10 Lee St • 9281 9666 • Dis access • Air conditioning • $–$$ • www.yha.com.au*

3 wake up!
If your plan for Sydney is all action, this is the place for you. It offers special cushion rooms for watching TV, colour-coded dorm walls and many other facilities. ⓢ *Map M6 • 509 Pitt St • 9288 7888 • Limited dis access • Air conditioning • $$ • www.wakeup.com.au*

4 Formule 1 Kings Cross
You can count on rooms being spick and span at this reliable budget motel chain. All accommodate three people for the flat room rate, most with a queen and single bunk bed. There's a TV but not much else. ⓢ *Map P4 • 191–201 Williams St, Kings Cross • 9326 0300 • Dis access • En-suite • Air conditioning • $$ • www.formule1.com.au*

5 Wattle House
It's pretty, quiet and clean, offering a good kitchen, library, courtyard and fours, twins and double rooms. The 1877 house has been restored and guests have access to it 24-hours. ⓢ *Map J5 • 44 Hereford St, Glebe • 9552 4997 • $–$$ • www.wattlehouse.com.au*

6 Noah's Bondi
Spectacular views come at only a tiny premium at this friendly, recently-renovated hostel. The rooms and bathrooms are clean and Noah's staff speak Japanese and Hebrew. ⓢ *Map H5 • 2 Campbell Parade, Bondi Beach • 9365 7100 • $ • www.noahsbondibeach.com*

7 Billabong Gardens
Billabong offers both motel and hostel accommodation, a great kitchen and a swimming pool. The amiable owners also specialise in helping backpackers to find work. ⓢ *Map C5 • 5–11 Egan St, Newtown • 9550 3236 • $–$$ • www.billabonggardens.com.au*

8 Palisade
At this cherished institution in the heart of The Rocks you'll be torn between the cosy local pub downstairs, the justly praised dining room upstairs and harbour views from some of the rooms. ⓢ *Map D3 • 35 Bettington St, Millers Point • 9247 2272 • No dis access • $$ • www.palisadehotel.com.au*

9 Manly Bungalow
A classic Manly house has been converted into an eight-room guesthouse, surrounded by tropical plants and an outdoor entertaining area. It's close to the ocean beach and to the ferry wharf. Each room has a kitchenette, there's a shared laundry, and week-long rates are available. ⓢ *Map U3 • 64 Pittwater Rd, Manly • 9977 5494 • $–$$ • www.manlybungalow.com*

10 Waldorf Woolloomooloo
Studio apartments in this serviced complex are excellent value and good for families. They can sleep up to five people and have full kitchens and living areas. The walk to the city through the Botanic Gardens is lovely. ⓢ *Map P4 • 88 Dowling St, Woolloomooloo Bay • 8837 8000 • Dis access • En-suite • Air conditioning • $$$ • www.woolloomooloo-waldorf-apartments.com.au*

Price Categories

For a standard double room per night (with breakfast if included), taxes and extra charges.	**$** under $80
	$$ $80–150
	$$$ $150–250
	$$$$ $250–350
	$$$$$ over $350

Lobby at Medina Executive Sydney Central

🔟 Serviced Apartments

1 Quay West Suites Sydney

Luxurious, fully-equipped apartments with five-star service. Spacious suites have all the standards plus two TVs, stereos, fax and modem ports, deluxe minibar, valet and 24-hour room service. Choose from city or harbour views. ✎ Map M2 • 98 Gloucester St, The Rocks • 9240 6000 • No dis access • $$$–$$$$ • www.mirvac hotels.com

2 Medina Executive Sydney Central

Housed in one of Sydney's most beautiful buildings, the former Parcel Post Office, Medina's apartments are stylishly furnished. There are work areas as well as living and dining spaces, great kitchens, cable TV and stereos. ✎ Map M6 • 2 Lee St, Haymarket • 8396 9800 • $$$$–$$$$$ • www. medina.com.au

3 Waldorf

Reasonably priced and well-located, the Waldorf has facilities such as a rooftop pool, spa and sauna, complimentary in-house movies and a shopping service. ✎ Map M5 • 57 Liverpool St • 9261 5355 • No dis access • $$$ • www. waldorf.com.au

4 The York

This hotel is ideally located close to several tourist attractions and transport links. Its refurbished apartments have balconies and good facilities. ✎ Map M2 • 5 York St • 9210 5000 • No dis access • $$$$ • www. theyorkapartments.com.au

5 Medina on Crown

Close to the groovy Crown Street shops and restaurants, Sydney Cricket Ground and Fox Studios, this hotel is also right above the legendary restaurant Bills (see p60). ✎ Map N6 • 359 Crown St, Surry Hills • 8302 1000 • $$$$–$$$$$ • www. medina.com.au

6 Hotel Stellar

This newly-renovated hotel is good value for families, there is no extra charge for kids under 12, and two bedroom apartments have a queen and four bunk beds. The rooms are large but only three apartments have fully equipped kitchens. ✎ Map N5 • 4 Wentworth Ave • 9264 9754 • No dis access • $$–$$$$ • www. hotelstellar.com

7 Morgans of Sydney

Situated on one of Darlinghurst's prime eat streets, this art deco boutique hotel is walking distance to Potts Point and Paddington. Check out the roof terrace for views to the Opera House and Harbour Bridge. ✎ Map E4 • 304 Victoria St, Darlinghurst • 9360 7955 • No dis access • $$$ • www.morganshotel.com.au

8 Meriton Bondi Junction

Built above the Bondi Junction bus and train interchange, these bedroom apartments have views of Sydney Harbour or the ocean. Great features include full-sized kitchens and laundries, pools and tennis courts. ✎ Map F5 • 95–97 Grafton St, Bondi Jnctn • 9287 2890 • No dis access • $$$ • www. meritonapartments.com.au

9 Quest Grande Esplanade

A smart, modern apartment hotel, where many rooms look over a row of pine treees onto Manly's harbour beach. It is also close to dozens of restaurants and cafés. ✎ Map U3 • 54a West Esplanade, Manly • 9976 4600 • $$$ • www.quest grandeesplanade.com.au

10 Manly Seaside Holiday Apartments

This agency rents 134 fully self-contained apartments in a range of buildings around Manly. Perfect for longer stays, this is a great way to feel at home. Various types of accommodation are available, many with views, from budget to deluxe in all sizes. ✎ Map U3 • 2/39 East Esplanade, Manly • 9977 5213 • No dis access • Some air conditioning • $–$$$ • www.manly-seaside.com

Unless otherwise stated, all apartments accept credit cards, have en-suite bathrooms and air conditioning and provide dis access.

149

General Index

→

Acknowledgements

The Authors

Steve Womersley has lived in Sydney on and off since childhood. He has worked with some of the world's leading travel publishers as a writer and editor and currently lives in country Victoria.

Steve Womersley would like to thank Jane Fuller, Mickey Morelle, Terri Dylan and Terry Harding for their hospitality, Gerry Gallagher, Terry Stuart, Stephanie Holt, Peter Anderson, Rachel Neustein, Loren Polzot and Anita Krivickas for their insider tips, and Sera Jane and Minka for their patience.

Born in Paddington, Rachel Neustein has always lived in inner Sydney and knows all the back alleys and secret spots. She writes about art, fashion, film, food and music for various Australian and international magazines.

Rachel Neustein would like to thank Damien Power, Nell Heard, Alice Addison and David N Reginald.

Photographer Carol Wiley
Additional Photography
Shaen Adey, Max Alexander, Simon Blackall, Andy Crawford, Frank Greenaway, Dave King, Eddie Lawrence, Diana Lynn, David Murray, Michael Nicholson, Siobhan O'Connor, Rob Reichenfeld, Sanjay Sharma, Clive Streeter, Alan Williams

DK INDIA

Managing Editor Aruna Ghose
Art Editor Benu Joshi
Project Editor Anees Saigal
Project Designer Divya Saxena
Senior Cartographer Uma Bhattacharya
Cartographer Suresh Kumar
Picture Researcher Taiyaba Khatoon
DTP Co-ordinator Shailesh Sharma
DTP Designer Vinod Harish
Fact Checker Kelly Adams
Indexer Bhavna Seth Ranjan

DK LONDON

Managing Editor Fay Franklin
Publishing Manager Jane Ewart
Senior Cartographic Editor Casper Morris
Senior DTP Designer Jason Little
Production Linda Dare
DK Picture Library Romaine Werblow, Hayley Smith, Gemma Woodward
Additional Contributors Emma Anacootee, Claire Baranowski, Julie Bond, Ellen Root, Ros Walford, Carol Wiley, Hugo Wilkinson

Picture Credits

t-top, tl-top left; tlc-top left centre; tc-top centre; tr-top right; cla-centre left above; ca-centre above; cra-centre right above; cl-centre left; c-centre; cr-centre right above; clb-centre left below; cb-centre below; crb-centre right below; bl-bottom left, b-bottom; bc-bottom centre; bcl-bottom centre left; br-bottom right; d-detail.

Every effort has been made to trace the copyright holders, and we apologize in advance for any unintentional omissions. We would be pleased to insert the appropriate acknowledgements in any subsequent edition of this publication.

The publisher would also like to thank the following for their kind assistance and permission to photograph their establishments:
Angsana Spa, ARQ Sydney, Australian Museum, Bank Hotel, Bar Colluzi, Bather's Pavillion Cafe, Belle Fleur, Bill and Toni's, Bit Brasserie, Brett Whiteley Studio, Café Mint, Café Sydney, Chelsea Hotel, Coffee Culture, C's Flashback, Dive, Dinosaur Designs, East Ocean, Elizabeth Bay House, Fifi's, Gleebooks, Golden Century, Guillaume at Bennelong, Hambledon Cottage, Historic Houses Trust, Hyde Park Barracks, Imperial Hotel, Jan Logan, Justice & Police Museum, Kirketon, The Legislative Assembly, 158 Lotus, Mambo Friendship Store, Manly Wharf Hotel, Mecca Cosmetica, Medina Executive Sydney Central, Medusa, Moorish, Nutcote, National Trust of Australia (NSW), Old Government House, Parramatta, Park Hyatt Sydney, Radisson Kestrel Manly, Red Lantern, Rothbury Estate Winery, Sailors' Home, State Theatre, Strand Arcade, Stellar Suites, Susannah Place Shop, Sydney Opera House, Sydney Visitors' Centre, Taronga Park Zoo, That Noodle Place, Tetsuya's Victorie, Welcome Hotel, Softiel Wentworth, The Westin Sydney.

Works of Art have been reproduced with the permission of the following copyright holders:
© Imants Tillers and Alec Tzannes *Dome of the Federation Pavillion (1985-87)* 38tc.
© MUSEUM OF SYDNEY 1996: *Edge of the Trees* (detail), Janet Laurence and Fiona Foley, on the site of the First Government House 47tr, 47br.
© ART GALLERY OF NEW SOUTH WALES Grace Cossington-Smith, *The Lacquer Room*, 1935-1936, oil on paperboard on plywood, 74 »

90.8cm, Purchased 1967, Collection: Art Gallery NSW © AGNSW, photograph: Christopher Snee for AGNSW [accn# DA10.1967] 25tl; Edward Poynter, *The Visit of the Queen of Sheba to King Solomon*, 1890, oil on canvas, 234.5 x 350 x 20.5 cm frame, Purchased 1892, Collection: AGNSW, photograph: Ray Woodbury for AGNSW, accn# 898] 24cb; Hans Hasenpflug, *Rhapsody in Satin*, 1937 gelatin silver photograph, vintage, 30.2 x 37.8cm, Gift of Mr Christopher Hamilton the artist's son 1984, Collection: Art Gallery of NSW [accn# 182.1984], 25cra; *Amitabha Buddha*, late 8thC–mid 9thC, andesite, 105 x 88 x 65cm, Purchased with funds provided by the Art Gallery Society of New South Wales 2000, Collection: Art Gallery NSW, photograph: Jenni Carter for AGNSW accn# 144.2000] 24br.

© Wendy Whiteley 1996, *The Balcony 2*, 1975, Brett Whiteley (1939-92), oil on canvas, 203.5 x 364.5cm 27b, Collection: Art Gallery of NSW.

© NATIONAL GALLERY OF VICTORIA, MELBOURNE, AUSTRALIA Eugene von Guerard, born Austria 1811, worked in Australia 1852-81, died England 1901, *Sydney Heads* 1860, oil on canvas, 48.5 x 76.3 cm, Purchased through The Art Foundation of Victoria with the assistance of Roslyn and Kerry Packer, Founder Benefactors, 1986 27crb.

© AUSTRALIAN NATIONAL MARITIME MUSEUM COLLECTION, reproduced courtesy of the museum 36tl, 42c

The publishers would like to thank the following individuals, companies and picture libraries for their kind permission to reproduce their photographs.

ALAMY IMAGES: Kerry Dunstone 21cb; Nigel Luckhurst, Lebrecht Music Collection 65tr; Christine Osborne, Worldwide Picture Library 94 br; Sergio Pitamitz 14-15c; Slick Shoots 2Gala; David Gouth 77tr.

ART GALLERY OF NEW SOUTH WALES: 25bc.
AUSTRALIAN CHAMBER ORCHESTRA: Photographer: Stephen Oxenbury 04bl, 06l.
AUSTRALIAN INFORMATION SERVICE: 37tl.
AUSTRALIAN MUSEUM, Sydney: 42tl.

BARZURA CAFÉ: 101bl.
NIC BEZZINA: 67tl.
CLOTH: 94bc.
CORBIS: David Ball 130-131;
P. Caron 52tl; Michelle Chaplow 12clb, 49tr, 52bl; L. Clarke, CRDPHOTO 1c; Graeme Goldin, Cordaiy Photo Library 34-35c; John Van Hasselt, CORBIS SYGMA 64tc, 71tr, 72tl; Jose Fusta Raga 4-5; Nick Rains, Cordaiy Photo Library 17cr, 72tr; Bill Ross 28-29c; Royalty Free 73tr; Paul A. Souders 45tr, 26t.
LUNA PARK SYDNEY: 56t, 115tr.
JACQUELINE MITELMAN 40bl.
By Permission of the NATIONAL LIBRARY OF AUSTRALIA: Portrait of Henry Lawson / Paramount, [190-?], gelatin silver, 27.9 x 20.3 cm, nla.pic-an23351980 40tr;
© Greg Weight.1946-. Portrait of Brett Whiteley (Detail), 1976, gelatin silver on fibre-based paper, image 45.6 x 31 cm, on sheet 50.5 x 40.6 cm, nla.pic-an12090936 26tl; John Olsen with painting *"The bath"* (Detail), 1997, gelatin silver, image 35.3 x 42.5 cm and 17.9 x 22.5cm, nla pic-an21100990 26tc;v
© Mrs. Ann Mills, *Self Portrait* (Detail) Grace Cossington-Smith 26tr.
MANLY BUNGALOWS: 148tr.
MASTERFILE: R. Ian Lloyd 74-75.
MITCHELL LIBRARY, STATE LIBRARY OF NEW SOUTH WALES 36tc, 36tr, 36bc, 37tr, 37br.
NILGIRI'S: 119tl.
OPERA BAR: 68tr.
POWERHOUSE MUSEUM: 7clb, 30c, 30cla, 30bl, 31cr, 31bl, 42bl.
SOFITEL WENTWORTH SYDNEY: 145tl.
SYDNEYATTRACTIONSGROUP: 28bl.
Courtesy of the SYDNEY OPERA HOUSE: 3tc, 8-9c, 8tl, 8br, 9bc, 10tl, 10tr, 11t, 11c, 11cr.
SYDNEY WILDLIFE WORLD: 29cr.
STATE LIBRARY OF NEW SOUTH WALES: 10cra, 16tl.
TARONGA PARK ZOO: 33cr, 33b.
THE BOOKSHOP DARLINGHURST: 76tl.
WILDFIRE: 58tc, 58c.
ZIMMERMANN PADDINGTON: 94tr.

All other images are © Dorling Kindersley. For further information see www.dkimages.com.

Selected Street Index